DANCING WITH ELVES

PARENTING AS A PERFORMING ART

THE PARENTS' HANDBOOK OF
PARENTING STRATEGIES

By

JOHN GALL, MD, FAAP

ISBN: 1-4107-2316-X (e-book)
ISBN: 1-4107-2317-8 (Paperback)

Library of Congress Control Number: 2003091500

This book is printed on acid free paper.

Printed in the United States of America
Bloomington, IN

1stBooks - rev. 03/15/03

CONTENTS

PREFACE

Elegant Parenting: Strategies for the Twenty-First Century appeared in 1994. Some friends, noticing that the book weighed over two pounds, asked for something lighter, something they could read in an hour or two and then carry around in their pocket for reference. This book is the result of that request. Stripped down to essentials, it nevertheless contains the substance, including all but one or two of the sixty-some strategies, of the larger book.

Like its predecessor, this book is an attempt to make a constructive contribution to a world where improvement in the quality of human interactions may be a deciding factor for our very survival as a species. We must learn how to interact better with our fellow human beings. And the most crucial situation is the parenting relationship, where the skills and habits and expectations of the next generation are being formed through actual experience.

Some—including some child care specialists—may feel that it is a mistake to put such potent tools into the hands of parents who lack lengthy professional training. Our reply is that no one can avoid influencing others. The only question is whether we are going to do it knowingly or unknowingly. Our position is that knowledge is better than ignorance.

If you as a parent diligently study and practice the techniques in this book you may reach that point where you don't even have to think about parenting any more. It's not an issue, it's not a problem area. It's just a dance, equally satisfying to everyone involved. At that point you can congratulate yourself on your mastery of Parenting as a Performing Art.

1.

INTRODUCTION: THE BASICS

The first thing to know about Parenting is: it's a dance. Newborn babies can't speak English or Spanish when they're born, but they can dance. And they know it when you are dancing. You can stand in front of a little baby and move your arms and shoulders just a little bit, in rhythm, and you will see their eyes widen as they pick up on it, they may smile and if they're feeling good, they'll give it right back to you. You have sent them a message that says, "Baby, let's dance!" and they have replied, "I dig you Momma, I'm dancing."

You don't have to move very much. They pick it up if you just tilt your head a little from side to side. That tells them you're dancing. You don't even have to move your body at all. You can do it with your voice. You put that little singsong in it and their body starts to dance to your tune. And they love it. You're telling them they're born to dance and life is a dance. It's going to be OK.

You hold them in your arms and you do that gentle back and forth movement and they know you're dancing with them.

If you've ever seen one of those people who jiggle babies too fast in their arms, they're not being in rhythm, they're putting their own pressure into the dance—babies don't like that. They're telling them life could be a dance but it's all tensed up, all up tight. Bad message!

So you learn how to dance gracefully, in rhythm and at the proper tempo and you learn to do it with your voice and your eyes as well as your body and you practice that, because it makes your own life a smoother dance, too.

You practice it, over and over, until you get really good at it.

Default Mode

Now this is the computer age and I think most of you know what Default Mode is. It's what the computer does when you don't give it any specific instructions. You open up a page, you start to type, and everything you type is in Geneva typeface size 10. Your computer has a hundred different typefaces in it and if you don't tell it what to do, it picks Geneva size 10. You could have had Old English Bold size 14 if you had thought about it, but you didn't ask and so you didn't get. When the computer doesn't know what to do, it goes to Default Mode where it keeps the instructions that were put into it when it was still on the assembly line.

People are like this, too. If somebody says, Good morning! to you, you automatically say back to them, Good morning! Or if you aren't feeling good, if you're in a mean mood, you can say something else back to them. You can say, What do you mean, good? Those are your wired-in instructions, those are your Default Mode responses, to use automatically if you're feeling good or if you're not feeling so good.

But let's say the person coming up to you is your Aunt Sally and you really don't want to talk to Aunt Sally because Aunt Sally will talk all day and drive you crazy and what you want is for her to just go away right now, but you can't say, Get out of here! because she's your Aunt Sally. Then you start to think a little before you speak and you remember something. You say, "Oh Hello, Aunt Sally! I just saw your sister go around the corner there looking for you cause she's got some juicy gossip to tell you and if you hurry you can just catch her up."

When you do that, you're not in Default Mode any more. You're putting some thought into your speech. You're choosing your words deliberately to achieve a specific goal. You're using a strategy. You are now in charge of getting the kind of outcomes that you want. You are taking charge of the situation, you are making it come out the way you want it to come out. You're not willing to just run on automatic and say whatever is in your own Default Mode and get stuck with whatever happens as a result of that.

Once you start doing that, you begin to taste the sweet taste of success, of power over your own interactions with others.

Default Mode is so limiting. If you're like many people, you have a Default Mode that tells you that if somebody doesn't go along with what you want, you can whine or nag, or get mad or threaten them, or say, Forget you. And pretty soon you're living a life that's nothing but whining and nagging, and getting mad and threatening and then trying to deal with the negative reactions you're getting from other people and you're wondering why Fate is so cruel to you. But if you start to analyze the situation and figure it out, you realize that you did it yourself, you produced those reactions yourself by operating out of Default Mode, just running on automatic and not using your power to pick and choose your own interaction strategies.

And especially when you're dealing with a newborn baby or a little child, you can't just blast away in Default Mode. You've got to put some thought into your interactions. And it really helps to know what kinds of interactions are likely to get you what you want. It really helps to have a list that you can turn to, that you can pick and choose from and pick one that's likely to work. That's what this book is for, to help you build up that list for yourself.

Basics

Communication with a baby or a toddler or a small child is special in several ways. You're not dealing with an equal, you're dealing with a very special little person whose whole future depends on how well you as an adult can communicate with that little person. You can't use power plays and get away with it. You can't make assumptions and expect the little person to fill in what you fail to make clear. You can't expect them to have understanding beyond their developmental level. And if you don't know what can be expected at each developmental level, you must find that out because the child cannot tell you what the child himself or herself does not know. So communicating with a baby or a child carries with it a greater responsibility than does communicating with another adult.

You step into their world, you dance with them in their world, and you do it in such a way that they are meeting their goals even as you are achieving your own goals.

They are not in this world in order to live up to your expectations. They are here to become who they are destined to be. If you want something from them, you must make sure it helps them advance toward their own goals. Otherwise it just won't work.

Developmental Level

You do need to know the developmental level of the child if you want to meet them at their own level of understanding and behavior. And it may seem like a huge task to read the forty volumes of Piaget or the extensive writings of Erik Erikson. But I want to remind you that each and every one of us has already personally had experience, in our own childhood lives, of each and every one of those developmental stages. This is knowledge that we already have but don't know we have, and if you can tap into that, you can meet a child at his or her own level without having read everything in the world on child development. I'm not suggesting that you *not* read Piaget, I just want you to know that there's a lot you can do anyway.

Utilization

Of course you adapt your parenting to the developmental level of the child. That goes without saying. But you can go much farther than that. You can actively utilize those developmental thrusts, that impetus, that momentum, so that Mother Nature provides the motive power to help you get where you want to go. When the baby gets so interested in the food on mother's plate that she pulls off the breast and falls into the plate, you know that you can introduce solid foods because the child is actively interested, she's ready for that next stage. And when your toddler compulsively begins to explore every cupboard in the house, you don't stop them, you praise them for being such a good explorer. You make the house safe, and you watch them closely so you can save their life if necessary, and then you let them explore. You just stand out of the way of a spontaneous process that has a lot of active drive behind it. As Buckminster Fuller used to say: Don't oppose forces—utilize them. If you follow this principle you will find that child-rearing has very little of nay-saying in it. You won't be chasing the child around telling them not to do things, you'll be watching with satisfaction as the child's instinctive drives cause them to spontaneously do the very things you wanted them to learn to do.

You will also find that the skill you develop in communicating with a child will vastly improve your skill in communicating with other adults, because most of our problems in communicating with other adults are due to our lack of practice and lack of repertoire in basic skills of communication generally,

Now, I've stressed that communicating with little ones is special and now that I've gotten that point across, I want to go back and emphasize the other side of the picture and that is that the basics are the same. Communication is communication and the basics are the same.

Verbal and Nonverbal

When you communicate with someone, you are sending them messages not just verbally but also nonverbally, not just by your words but also by your entire selfhood. Your tone of voice, your posture, your body language, your facial expression, how fast you talk, when you talk, the circumstances and situations in which you talk, and a million other things that we don't often think of as communication—all of those are messages that go right along with the verbal message and often speak far louder than our words. If you want to have the effect on the other person that you are hoping for, you must learn to be aware of the nonverbal components of your communication and master your ability to produce the specific nonverbal messages that you wish to be transmitted. You can't *not* communicate. You are always communicating whether you know it or not, so you may as well learn how to control your communications so you get what you want.

Tying Them Up in Nots

One of our greatest problems in communicating with children is the use of the word, "Not." We say to them: "Don't do this," and their mind makes a picture of of themselves doing whatever "this" is. When we think of *not* falling off the bicycle what we are really doing is making tiny microscopic movements of all the muscles involved in actually falling off the bicycle, and if we get distracted at that moment, we actually do fall off the bicycle. So when you tell your kids not to do things—all that does is make it more likely that they will at some future time slip and do those things. What you do is give them a positive command. You say: "Stop!" You say: "Freeze!" Every living creature knows how to do that. Or better yet, you go non-verbal. You throw up your arms and shriek. That will even stop a toddler in his tracks. Later on, when their verbal skills are more developed, you can discuss *not* doing things. But even then, thinking in terms of negatives is tricky business.

Yes and No

So remember verbal and nonverbal, and remember compliance versus resistance. Every child, every person has two attitudes, one of compliance and the other of resistance. One part wants to obey and be in harmony with you, the other part wants to resist you and be a distinct and separate person by rejecting what comes from outside. If you give a request and the person is mainly in compliance mode, they will likely be happy to do what you suggest. If they are mainly in resistance mode, they are likely to push back against your request.

My point is, it is up to you as an adult with superior wisdom and knowledge of the world to recognize when a child is in compliance mode and when they are in resistance mode, and when they are somewhere in between. It's not up to them to tell you, they don't even know about such things. But they will signal it to you, and you really ought to learn how to read those signals. Otherwise you will be spending a lot of time trying to force compliance after you have given the wrong form of request. When a child is in resistance mode, you structure your communication in such a way that

7

they can succeed in resisting you. You thus give them the success that every person needs and must have in order to feel like a competent human being, while at the same time you have achieved what you wanted to achieve. They will proudly prove to you that they can so do it, and you can be very surprised and admit that you were wrong, they really are big enough to carry out the garbage. So what if they spill, so what if they don't do it as well as you can? You allow them that success and you don't mess it up by criticising their performance. Later on, they'll do it even better.

Repertoire

That brings me to the topic of repertoire. You know that if you want to be a good musician or a good auto mechanic, or a good anything, you have to master a certain number of basic techniques. You've got to know how to play your instrument in tune, you've got to know the musical scales, you have to know how to play louder and softer, and so on. You have to have a repertoire of basic techniques. And in music, if you want to perform in public, you have to literally have a repertoire, you have to know at least a couple of pieces that you can perform by heart, that you know so well you can play them even when you're not in peak form. How many of you saw the movie "Amadeus?" You remember, Mozart was so good that he could play a piece of music backwards. In one amazing scene, his friends held his body upside down while he played a piece on the piano with his hands over his head. That's what I call repertoire!

It's the same with parenting strategies. You have to practice them until you can do them off-the-cuff, spontaneously, automatically.

The Ten Thousand Year Old Strategy

In human communication, repertoire means that you know at least twenty or thirty or forty different ways of interacting with another human being. It was a real shock to me when I realized that for two thousand years—longer than that—for ten thousand years—human beings have generally interacted with each other using only one strategy. One and only one. If you want another person to do something, you ask the other person to do it. You say, "Do it!" Sometimes you say, "Please do it," but that's the same basic strategy. If they don't do it, you may give up, or you may raise your voice and ask again. And if they still don't do it, you may start to put a little threat in your voice or offer a bribe, and after they have refused two or three times you threaten to knock their block off or never speak to them again, or to take some other action that you think would be a punishment to them. And this one strategy leads eventually to a threat to blow up the whole world. It's amazing! One strategy in universal use throughout the entire world for the whole of human history!

Some people say, "What do you mean, strategy? That's just human nature. That's reality. There isn't any other way." And I say to you, today is not too soon to begin to learn some of those other ways and to start enjoying the rewards of success in human interaction.

But there's a warning that goes with this: You cannot use power plays on little kids without having to suffer the consequences. There will be a reckoning even if it is delayed twenty years. There is a larger goal than obedience and that is the continued growth and development of your child's personality—his or her ability to become the loving, creative, and responsible human being you want him or her to be. So when I say this is a course in getting kids to do what you want—*that* is what I mean. Of course, we do want

9

some compliance, but above all else we want their own best interests.

Beyond Command-and Control.

In this new approach, children's behaviors are not treated as problems of discipline. They are treated very objectively, simply as a behavioral challenge for the caretaker to respond to in a constructive way.

Nor are they treated as problems of restraining the behavior of the child. No animal curbs the spontaneous behavior of its offspring except for matters of safety or when the offspring is interfering with the parent's nap.

We do have a restraining and controlling function as adults, but if we define our total relationship to our charges in those terms, we could just as well have hired a guard dog or a policeman. We are humans and our function is to help little humans grow up to be fully functioning adults.

In the old model—the one that's been around for ten thousand years—the emphasis is on command and control. You tell a person what to do and if they don't do it, you punish them in some way. The surprising thing is that this model inspires so much faith, since it really doesn't work very well. And it certainly is not cost-effective in the long run, because it entails a terrible price that is exacted later on in life.

Let's face it. If it really worked all that well, you wouldn't be reading this book!

Command-and-control tries to get 100% compliance— an impossible goal. In the name of discipline, it teaches rigidity. With the strategic approach, you try a strategy and if it doesn't work, you switch to another one. Any given strategy may work only ten percent of the time. That's OK, that's fine. You try another one. You don't try to force compliance. You keep switching.

In the new model the emphasis is on the web of human interactions. The key word is not control but strategies of interaction. The desired behavior is elicited not by a command, but by organizing the situation in such a way that the desired behavior occurs spontaneously.

That Other Child Abuse

Almost all of us grow up with a chronic disease, an unrecognized disease, called a Normal Childhood. I call it that to distinguish it from the grosser forms of child abuse that we all understand are wrong. Captain Kangaroo (Bob Keeshan) calls it, "That Other Child Abuse."He's referring to that unending stream of peremptory commands and harsh, demeaning words, threats, predictions of a bad end— we've all experienced it to some degree. We know what he's talking about. Its effects on our development and on our ability to learn correct ways of relating to other human beings can be devastating.

That's what Captain Kangaroo says, and I agree with him. The mad world we live in has been created by men and women reacting against and perpetuating the negative experiences of their own childhood. The failure of establishment psychiatry, and particularly the failure of psychoanalysis, to press this issue of so-called Normal Childhood or normal child abuse is one of the great failures of history.

It's clear that the founders of psychoanalysis knew. They spelled it out in case history after case history, but they drew back from naming the problem because to do so would be to indict the very methods of childrearing that the establishment regards as normal and necessary. To attack the concept of discipline? Impossible! To challenge the validity of punishment for wrongdoing? Absurd! To think that mere words can hurt a person permanently? Who would believe that?

11

So I'm throwing down the gauntlet right here and now. I am making a public wager of a hundred dollars. If any of my readers can bring me a documented example of even one of God's creatures other than human beings that uses punishment as part of their teaching of their offspring, I will pay that person a hundred dollars. I don't think I will have to pay. Now I'm perfectly aware that the mother wood duck pushes her babies out of the nest when they are a certain age, and I know that the mother raccoon pushes her babies into the water, forcing them to swim, if they hold back beyond a certain age, but these behaviors are not done as punishment. And I know that adult male sea lions torment and injure juveniles who come too close, and that male polar bears eat their babies.

None of this is done in a teaching situation.

In the springtime you can see the mother birds teaching their babies how to catch worms. The baby bird is in the grass, beak wide open, fluttering its wings, acting helpless—using the old strategy that used to work back up in the nest, but Momma bird isn't responding. She's right in front of her baby, pecking at the ground, pulling up worms and eating them, right in front of her baby. She keeps on doing this until baby bird finally copies her and pulls up a worm out of the ground for himself.

The mother bird repeats the sequence over and over, with endless patience, until the children learn. You never see a mother bird attack her offspring; you never see her punish a baby for failure to learn the lesson. When the adult animal teaches their offspring, it is done by one method only and that is by modelling over and over the desired behavior. They show them, over and over and over. Only human beings operate under the delusion that a child must be hurt in order to learn. It's in the earliest written records from ancient Egypt, it's in the Old Testament, it was taken for granted by St. Augustine in the Third Century AD, but it is wrong. It is wrong in the sense that it is ineffective. It works poorly. And it is counterproductive, because when that child grows up and gets into a position of power, even if it's only over the family dog, they are going to make someone else suffer what they had to suffer.

When you punish someone, you teach them how to be a punitive person. When you use a repertoire of constructive behavioral responses, you teach them how to do constructive responses. You model for them the very art of elegant human interaction.

The Naturalistic Approach

This approach has been given a name by that other famous Erickson, not Erik Erikson, but the psychiatrist Milton H. Erickson, M.D. He called it the Naturalistic approach. The basic principle underlying the Naturalistic approach to the child is respect for the integrity of the child—both physical and mental integrity—and for the child's view of the world. Naturally, the child's view is different from that of adults. The essence of the naturalistic approach is to pace into the child's view, rather than trying to force the adult's view onto the child. As Erickson himself put it:

> "No matter what the age of the child may be, there should never be any threat to the child as a functioning unit of society. Adult physical strength, intellectual strength, force of authority, and weight of prestige are all so immeasurably greater to the child than his own attributes that any undue use constitutes a threat to his adequacy as an individual." (1)

Children who have experienced this type of approach recognize that their individuality, their dignity, and their

13

need for comfortable interaction with the world have been respected, and their later behavior reflects this understanding.

Benevolent Curiosity

A year or so ago I was talking with a parents' group in Ann Arbor and someone asked me to boil it all down to one phrase. I think they were hoping that they could take home a magic phrase that would summarize and encapsulate this whole topic in some sort of verbal incantation. Well, as we talked about it, what finally emerged was the expression, "benevolent curiosity." We finally decided that the most productive parental attitude could be summed up as "benevolent curiosity." If our attitude is one of curiosity about the child's way of experiencing the world, coupled with a sustained attitude of support, interest, and well-wishing, we are most likely to be successful in our long term goal of having the child grow up to be what they are destined to be—not what *we* want them to be, but what they, by their very nature, are destined to be. We are the gardeners, they are the plants. We are benevolently interested in what kind of growth and flowering they will display.

How do you foster a child to become what they are destined to be? As Joseph Campbell says, "You help the child to follow his bliss." When Bill Moyers asked Campbell, "How can those of us who are parents help our children recognize their bliss?" Campbell replied, "You have to know your child and be attentive to the child… you can see the eyes open and the complexion change."(2)

You too can learn to see their eyes open and their complexion change.

2.

DANCING WITH ELVES: THE MASTER STRATEGY

O wad some power the giftie gie us
To see oursels as others see us!

Dancing Together

With apologies to Robbie Burns, the problem is bigger than that. True, we need to master the art of seeing ourselves as others see us. But that's only the first step. The second step is to to learn how to see others *as they see themselves*, because then we can take that third step and deliberately present ourselves in such a way that we pace into the other person's world. At that point we have the power to cause the other person to want to make constructive changes without feeling that they are being pressured or advised or lectured or whatever from some outside source. They feel that we are dancing together.

So how do you do this? There are four steps:

Awareness.

I use this word awareness because there needs to be some word to describe that fundamental shift of orientation that shifts a person's primary attention away from the stuff that's going on in their own head and onto what's actually

15

happening in front of their eyes with the other person. You can't do strategic human interactions if you aren't noticing what's going on with the other person. And this isn't a small point. You really have to practice until it gets to be second nature.

Tracking

Tracking is what you do after you learn to be aware of what's happening with the other person. You track their reactions until you begin to get the drift of where they're headed.

Pacing

The third step is pacing. Pacing means stepping into their world, validating their view of things. And in the vast majority of cases you want to do Positive Connotation, which is accepting what they are doing as the natural and proper thing for them to be doing at that moment, even if it seems outrageous or off the wall to you as an adult.

I have a couple of sentences that I teach my parenting classes to memorize so they will get the idea of positive connotation.

"Oh, I see you are doing X. And you really like it, don't you?"

To make it even more emphatic, I give a specific example.

"Oh, I see you are putting your head in the toilet bowl. And you really like it, don't you?"

If you say this to a kid in that situation, you are very likely to get a grin and a nod.

Leading.

The next step after you have paced with positive connotation is Leading. You say, "I wonder if you could do it again?"

And the kid will almost certainly oblige. Then you say, "That was great. Can you do it again?"

There will come a time after a certain number of repetitions when the child will say, "No, that's plenty."

You have gotten them to stop putting their head in the toilet bowl by asking them to keep on doing it. They are validated and you are validated. Everybody wins.

Positive Connotation

There are two basic methods of interacting. One is confrontation, the other is pacing and leading. Pacing starts with something called positive connotation. If you don't learn anything else I want you to memorize that phrase, positive connotation. You start by accepting what they're doing.

Now we're not talking about reaching for the electric plug, OK? But in general, whatever it is they're doing, you start where they're at because obviously they're accepting their own behavior, and in their world view that behavior is the thing they should be doing. So you start with their picture of the world, you start by accepting it and then you suggest a little more of it, you do some of it yourself, and pretty soon they are not moving away from you, they're moving in parallel with you. Then you move out a little ahead of them, you're leading them. At that point you can lead them down the hill or even farther up, at which point they will often switch and come down the hill by themselves.

The Dance Of Interaction

In the dance of life, interaction and resting, interaction and resting, or socializing and being alone, they alternate. It's a pattern of involvement and then stepping back, involvement, stepping back. When you do that deliberately to match the other person's pattern, you are pacing with them.

With a newborn baby, when they're in intake mode and they're looking for your face, you interact with them, you smile, you coo, you play with them, whatever they like, whatever you like.

Face Approach

Most kids are pre-programmed so that the smiling face or anything that remotely approximates it is pleasant for them. They're highly visual and that's the visual configuration that makes them feel better. You can get a lot of mileage out of just deliberately putting on a smiling face. Moms will often do Face Approach to the baby, move their face up close and then move back—and then move up again.

Then comes the moment when you find that they're not looking at you. That's the moment to back off, because they need a little time to themselves. They need to integrate the experiences that they have just had, they need to make a memory of that happy time. You give them that break, and it may last one second or two seconds or five seconds or they may fall asleep; but usually it's just a couple of seconds and then the next thing you know they are looking in your face again, so you interact again, and, after a few seconds of interaction, lo and behold, they're looking away, so you back off and give them a little time to themselves, and then interact a little again.

All of life is like this—interaction and then stepping back. That's the way human beings operate. You can't do 100% one thing straight through for 8 hours a day, and then turn it off for 16 hours. Industrial civilization thinks that we can function that way, but we don't, we have to have those breaks, coffee breaks, those moments of inattention, what's called daydreaming. Daydreaming is probably the most important thing that a human being does—because that's the time when all this stuff, this flood of experience, is integrated and organized and made meaningful in our lives. It's put away in such a way that it can be useful to us. It's useful for babies too.

It's the pacing that tells them that the other person really cares.

1. **Awareness** is that state of alertness where you know that there is such a thing as feedback and you are looking for it.
2. **Tracking** is noting your feedback in real time, moment by moment, to determine what is actually happening with the other person.
3. **Pacing** is when you use it to decide when to interact or to stop interacting, to dance with the other person. When you pace another person, whether it's a little baby or another adult, that other person feels comfortable, they feel security, because they're not being interrupted and confronted and forced to do something that is not spontaneous for them.

In the case of a newborn baby, you can register it objectively, as a slowing of the heart rate, and slower and deeper breaths and who knows how many thousands of biochemical, metabolic factors are involved. With a person who's old enough to give you verbal feedback, they'll tell you, "Gee, I feel so good around you, I really like to be with you, I always feel comfortable." That's what they say.

4. **Leading** is when you offer your own variation on the dance after you have joined them in their dance.

Yes Set

Sometimes, when I see a little kid in the waiting room and it's time for him to come in to the examining room, I ask: "Are you here today?"

And what's the answer to that question? There's no way they can say "No!" unless they just want to be contrary, in which case it's very easy then to jump into a Polarity strategy and play their game. But if the child says "Yes", then I will ask another question like, "Is your mommy with you today?"

"Yes."

"Are you walking towards my room?"

"Yes."

"Are you coming in the door?"

"Yes."

"Are you walking towards the stool?"

"Yes."

They really can't say "No" because these are absolutely, incontrovertibly "Yes" questions.

"Are you climbing on my table?"

"Yes."

By this time they often have a big grin on their face, because they've psyched out this game I'm playing with them.

"Are you sitting on the table?"

"Yes."

"Are you sticking out your tongue?"

"Yes."

Don't overuse it. Use it when it is beneficial for you and for the child. If it's used to exploit somebody, it will kick back and they'll get very, very leery. You don't want to break their sense of trust.

Compliance versus Resistance

They will stick out their tongue because of the momentum of those twenty consecutive "Yes" reactions that are in the dance. That's Compliance versus Resistance. But if they want to be resistant you just play it the other way. If you walk out and say, "Are you here today?" and they say, "No!" then you can say, "You don't want to come into my room!"

"Oh, yes I do!"

"You can't get up on my table, you're too little!"

"Ohhh, I am so big enough!"

"Well, I know you're too little to open your mouth."

"Ahhh!"

You can play the resistance. What you have to know is which is uppermost in the child at the time.

You Don't Want To Get Down, Do You?

One little kid was just raising Cain in the waiting room. Mom was carrying him. He was maybe 18 months, maybe 2 years old. I walked out into the waiting room and said, "You don't want to get down, do you? You don't want to go into the doctor's office, do you?" He did a double take, then there was this big grin, and he jumped down out of his mother's arms and ran into my examining room. Somebody understood him. Somebody agreed with his position. That's when they're willing to walk with you. You pace them, and then you lead.

That's the mark of a really good strategy, where it happens out of nowhere and nobody gets any credit for being the one who made anything happen. It's just totally woven into the web, it's not an intervention, it's just a spontaneous response.

Verbal Model

When you talk to a kid, you're using a verbal model of the universe. The child's verbal model is extremely limited. They may be able to say 500 words, or 5,000 words, but they haven't had very much experience, they don't know exactly where those labels apply in the outside world. When you try to change a kid's behavior through the verbal model, you're dealing with a relatively undeveloped resource.

You can use the verbal model to put a person into the Yes Set, but it works better if you use body language, too.

The resources that they really have well developed from birth on are the modeling resources—the direct modeling of what you do; that is to say, how you move your body and the expressions that you put on your face and the tone of your voice—the stuff that doesn't demand linguistic processing. You can get a kid to feeling good, just by looking like you're dancing. You can start a person to saying yes, by making tiny nodding movements of your head. You can put a child into what's called the Yes Mode or the Yes Set by modeling things that they spontaneously do, just by your own body movements.

Thirty-Three Patches Nonverbal Pacing)

(Heidi had a lazy eye and came home from the eye doctor with a patch over her good eye. She was really upset about having to go to daycare with an eye patch. When she got to the daycare she found thirty-three kids running around with patches on their eyes. She was the happiest girl in the world!

The teachers did it. While Heidi was at the doctor's office, they proceeded to cut out patches and have every kid at the daycare wear a patch. She was as happy as can be and wore that patch for the next 6 months.

They only did it for the one day. They never needed to do it again.

Now that's a truly elegant example of nonverbal pacing.

Good Explorers

When they're two years old and getting into everything, your job as a parent is to follow them around and save their life when necessary. When they start to investigate the fire in the fireplace, you move in fast and pick them up and save their life. But then—and this is the hard part—you praise them for being such a good explorer, such a good scientist with such a good curiosity. You don't chastise them for getting into things, you praise that spirit of exploration. You don't want to mess that up. You don't want to kill that spirit. Their task at the age of two years is to explore the world and learn as much as possible about the world around them and the way it works. They can only do that by exploration. It's your job to keep them alive, but you don't mess up their spirit of exploration.

"I'm Me!"

When they are three and their big developmental task is developing a sense of their own identity, they say "No" a lot because that's how they make themselves distinct from you. You don't attack that head-on and try to crush it. It's an essential developmental stage. You use the Polarity strategy a lot. You agree with them that they certainly don't want to use the potty just yet. That's for big boys. "You're only three. The potty is for big boys." That's all you have to say. You let the matter drop. If you see them actually trying out the potty, you stay very neutral, you don't praise them, because that would make it Mom's thing. You just say, "Oh, I see you are on the potty," and you keep on doing whatever you are doing. If they want your help they can ask for it.

No Help Luke!

One little guy in my practice was so afraid his Mom was going to help him do things that he used to yell at her, the very instant she started to move toward him, "No help Luke! No help Luke!" It was a matter of principle with him that Mom was not to help him unless he asked for it.

Scaredy-cat

You can even use pacing with things that are usually considered to be character traits, like shyness. You just get more shy than they are. You become the one who is afraid to go into a room full of people, you become the one who doesn't want to go outside today because it's too scary. You just pace right along higher and higher until eventually they reach the point where it's too much even for them.

"Mom, you're just a scaredy-cat!"

3.

NATURAL CONSEQUENCES

Toddlers fall a lot. It's part of learning to walk. Usually, it's just a sudden sit-down. They don't blame anybody, they just get up and try again. Falling is a natural consequence of not doing it right, and they know that, so they keep on practicing until they get it right.

Toddlers understand natural consequences. They know it's up to them. They're not being punished. If they want to stop falling, it's up to them. They have to take corrective action. They have to change their own behavior.

Even a tiny baby understands natural consequences. If the pacifier falls out of their mouth, they reach for it and replace it. If they are too young to reach and grasp, they make searching movements with their head and mouth.

Now if they are trying to do something that's really too hard for them and they keep failing, they may decide to do something else, or give up, or have a temper tantrum. But the main strategy (taking corrective action) has such a high rate of success in such a myriad of situations that it usually becomes automatic and ingrained. A lot of our behavior in life consists of automatic, almost-unconscious corrective actions. It acquires the quality of common sense. It gets to be taken for granted. There's not a lot of emotion connected with it, except the sense of satisfaction when it works as expected.

If a parent can provide a consequence that is perceived by the child as a natural consequence of what the child just did, the child may simply try to take some corrective action. In such a case, there is not a lot of emotion involved, and certainly no blaming. The child corrects the behavior that produced the undesired consequence and experiences the sense of satisfaction that comes with success. It's essential that the parent not deliberately contrive the consequence. In that case, it isn't "natural" at all. It's an artificially contrived negative consequence, and that, by definition, is a punishment.

The Punishment Trap

It's really important to remember that it must not be considered punishment. Punishment leads to the desire to get back, to get even. Or the child may decide he's just inferior, maybe even born bad and worthy of nothing better than punishment. You don't want that. And the child who has real spirit and defends his freedom the most is likely to be the guy that gets the most punishment. So you want to stay out of the punishment trap.

Let Them Make Some Mistakes

Mothers sometimes ask me, when their little babies are only a few weeks or months old, whether they should let their babies have two ounces or three ounces or four ounces of formula at each feeding. They are thinking in terms of calories, they have heard something about the number of fat cells or whatever the latest theory of obesity is, and they want to prevent their child from becoming obese or predisposed to obesity. I tell them to be sure to put more in the bottle than their child can possibly take and to let them work on that bottle until they stop drinking and press their lips together and shake their head "No."

In that way the child learns that they are in charge of their own intake. No one is holding out on them or rationing them, there is plenty available, and they must consult with their own internal appetite standards to find out when to stop. They learn to pay attention to their own internal reference standard, which is always available. And the habit of listening to that inner voice, that inner standard, that's the true meaning of discipline—self-regulation, self-control.

You teach a child internal control by allowing them to make wrong decisions. You set it up so that their wrong decisions don't result in loss of life or limb, but you allow them to make those decisions for themselves.

A great deal more is involved here than just letting a child feel more free from parental control. Mistake-making is the way the child gets to experience impersonal feedback; i.e., natural consequences, and thus learns something about the real world. When a parent is constantly controlling the child's behavior through rules, the child mainly experiences a world of rules and never gets a good reality check, because they never get a chance to bump up against the natural consequences. They don't learn to use natural feedback.

As part of this strategy, you learn to ignore unimportant stuff. Don't treat everything as equally important. In other words, you let them do quite a bit of what some people call misbehaving, that is, you let them make a lot of mistakes. If it isn't a matter of life and death or fundamentals, you let them do it and find out for themselves what the consequences might be.

Praise The Achievement, Don't Criticize The Shortcoming

You always praise the achievement! You praise the achievement, you don't criticize the shortcoming. If they button up their jacket wrong, you can say, "Wow, you really know how to button your jacket!" You can also say, "What's this extra buttonhole?" You're not criticizing, you're just curious and he can have the satisfaction of telling you about it. You can learn from him, and he can teach you.

The Pattern Of Success

That pattern of success is so important. Unless it's a matter of life or death, you don't interrupt it even if it's not what you had on your own agenda.

You've heard the old saying, "Accentuate the positive." It's seriously true. When you interact with a kid, try to stay at least 95% positive.

What Is Discipline, Really?

Now about this thing called "discipline:" The word "discipline" can have two meanings. It can mean submitting to external control. It can mean internal control. The kind of discipline we are concerned with here is internal control. Some parents want to force the child to exercise internal control. That's a contradiction in terms. Outside pressure to coerce internal control. If the child yields to the outside pressure, it's not internal control. So the child resists the outside pressure in order to preserve his internal control. The parents then escalate the outside pressure and the child becomes panicky, thinking he is going to be forced to give up his internal control of his own life. He is fighting desperately to preserve what the parents say they want him to exercise, but when he exercises it they put more pressure on him to give it up. A double bind—the child loses either way. He has to make a choice but both choices are wrong. If a child is brought up in this way it's not surprising that as an adult he or she may be seriously confused about what discipline and internal control are really all about.

Often, when people say "I had to discipline my child," they are actually punishing their child. Real discipline occurs when the child changes his own behavior in response to natural consequences.

I'm Outlasting Her, Thanks!

Dora was at the store with her Mom when she decided she was gonna play "Peeks" with the clothes racks. She went into the clothes racks and stood in one of them and yelled, "Peek!" Her Mom was supposed to come find her. Great place to play. Mom got tired of the game real fast and said, "You have to stay with me." Dora started screaming in frustration.

People started gathering around and staring but Mommy just smiled and said to the onlookers, "I'm outlasting her, thanks!"

Dora sat on the floor and kicked and screamed and had a fit. Finally she looked up and noticed the group of people around her, staring, and her face changed. She suddenly became embarrassed. She quit screaming and never did it again.

Her mother just let her experience the natural consequences of what she was doing.

The Worst Tantrum In The World

One winter a few years ago a little girl confided in her grandmother. She said, "Tomorrow, I'm gonna throw the worst tantrum in the world for Mommy."

She was mad because Mommy and Daddy were coming to our parenting class. They were coming because they had a four year old who was a true holy terror. This little girl calculated how to get her mother's goat, how to get everybody's goat.

The parents picked their kids up after the class and went home. After the grandmother was sure the kids had gone to sleep, she called the parents on the phone and told the mother what the kid had said.

This little girl had a habit of not getting dressed to get on the bus for morning kindergarten. Then Mom would have to drive her in the car. Next morning she started pulling this trick. She wasn't dressed when the bus came. Mother just waved out the door, "Sorry, she's not ready! It's OK!" The kid was quite surprised that there wasn't a big fuss. She was running around nude in the house, just being obnoxious. Mother very calmly went and turned the thermostat down to sixty. She acted as though nothing had happened. She asked, "Are you going to have your breakfast?"

"No!"

"Oh, OK."

Mom went about her day's tasks. She put a sweater on herself and on the older child and proceeded through her morning routine, responding socially to the kid but not getting in any way upset or berating her in any way for not having her clothes on, acting as if this was perfectly normal, to run around all day without your clothes.

She took her down into the basement and spent a good bit of time down there where it was a lot colder, doing some laundry and a few things like that. Not a word, no berating or complaining. Around eleven thirty or so, the kid went upstairs and got her clothes on. The mother didn't say anything, she just went and turned the thermostat up again to a comfortable temperature.

They had also had hassles around lunch. Mother forgot to fix lunch. Nobody had any lunch and pretty soon the little girl said very politely, "Mother, I believe I'm ready for lunch now."

"Oh! Is that right? Well, OK. We're going to have such and such and such."

Not a complaint, nothing was said. They all had their lunch and it was very pleasant and this went on for the rest of the day. The kid quit doing any of those tantrums.

The next morning she got up, got dressed, and got on the bus, with no fuss about what she was going to eat or what she was going to wear. It was a one-shot cure.

Two Days and Nights of Wild Free Nakedness

You don't necessarily have to give the same response to the same problem. Laurel, four years old, fought being dressed. She just didn't want to put on any clothes, ever, so her Mom decided to let her stay undressed. She didn't scold her, she didn't guilt-trip her, she just said, "OK." Laurel spent two full days of wild, free nakedness, then decided she liked to be dressed. There has been no problem since. Why fight against the lure of the forbidden? Why not just let her find out that nakedness is nice, but clothes are better?

Clothes in the Car

Another Mom had trouble getting her kid dressed in the morning. Twice, within about two weeks, he went off in his pajamas to day care because he didn't care if he was dressed or not. The closer they got to day care, the more he started to care!

He got dressed in the car outside day care, twice, and not once since then.

Time To Hop Up And Run Around The House Three Times

Peter loved to get up several times during dinner and run around the house and then come back. Every time he came back his Mom gave him a hug and said how much she missed him. Then she started suggesting he run around the house after each bite of dinner. In a few days he gave the whole thing up. It was just too much.

A Very Strange Kind Of Helpfulness

You stay on their side, you are very understanding. You say, "Would you like to leave your clothes in the car, or would you like to take them with you?" You're helping them, but it's a very strange kind of helpfulness. You're letting the child's failure to learn the desired responses get in his way, not yours. It becomes a problem for him but not for you.

As you start to leave the house you suddenly draw back and say, "Oh, no! I forgot! We can't go to the ice cream shop because you guys always fight in the car!"

If they fight in the car, it's just a Natural Consequence that Mom and Dad can't take them to get ice cream. They hadn't been thinking of that when they fought. How can they convince you that they won't fight any more? It's really hard to prove a negative. They'll have to be really convincing. Now the burden of proof is on them. Fighting in the car has suddenly become a problem for them but not for you.

4.

THE INDIRECT APPROACH

Most of us haven't had much experience in indirectly directing other people's spontaneous attention. We've had a lot of experience in sitting in classrooms and hearing the command, "Pay attention!" So we tend to use that by telling our kids, "Pay attention!" But deliberately practicing the specific technical skill of indirectly directing another person's attention—we usually don't do that.

Toss the Towel

Let's say your daughter has spilled some milk on the kitchen floor. The direct approach would be to scold, or to instruct, or even to sympathize. But you could say nothing about it, just toss the towel to her while you're continuing the conversation. You imply, by your behavior, that a certain behavior is going to take place, and nine times out of ten it will. You haven't even asked them. They just do it—and they don't feel coerced. It even works for drying the dishes.

Too Clean for the Chicken Coop

I knew a little girl who lived on a farm. She used to wear her Sunday dresses a lot, even on weekdays, because she figured her parents were less likely to tell her to clean out the chicken house if she was all dressed up! She was using this powerful strategy of Indirection to shape the behavior of her parents! "Too Clean for the Chicken Coop"—that's what we decided to call it.

Book-Ball

In my own school days, back in the seventh grade, my English teacher, Mr. Bagby, started class with a big pile of textbooks on his desk. He stood by the desk, picked up a dozen books and started passing them out by literally throwing them to the students. There were books flying in all directions and we students had to really pay attention to catch the one aimed at us. Without even speaking a word, Mr. Bagby made it plain to all of us that we were in a fast-paced ball game and we would have to keep our eyes open if we wanted to keep up. We wanted to keep up! It was such a refreshing change from what we were used to.

He would say, "Write that word on the board!" and a piece of chalk would come flying our way. We felt like an infielder going for a double play.

And with reading assignments, he would say, "Now tomorrow you're going to be a radio announcer and I'm going to give you ninety seconds to get your message across and tell this class what it's all about."

We loved it and we really learned English.

Parallel Accessing.

This next strategy is just a little bit tricky, but it's very powerful and elegant and when you've practiced it a little bit and gotten good at it you can get a lot of satisfaction out of using it. It's called Parallel Accessing. And I think it's best taught by example.

Age.

Age is very important to a child, so you can start an interaction with a two-year-old by asking: "Are you two?"

And you will most likely get an answer like: "Two years old."

Or, "I'm two." They say it in a special kind of singsong that tells you it's still just verbal, they don't really have the concept of time, but you have made them feel important just by asking; and they feel competent just by being able to answer you. So it's a very satisfying interaction. You have told them they are important and competent without ever using those big words. You only asked them, "Are you two?"

With a three year old, there's often a big difference.

"I'm tha-ree years old."

You can hear the pride in their tone of voice. What they are saying is, "That's who I am."

It's a matter of identity. You are validating their identity.

With four, five, six, seven, it's different again. It's a matter of achievement, of status. They are older than mere three-year-olds.

Now, with a girl: "Are you nine years old?"

"Oh, yes."

"Are you nine years and six months?"

You can see the sudden blink, the quick inward search, the mental calculation.

"Yeeaah." There's puzzlement. What is this all about?

"Are you nine years and six months and four days old?"

Blank smile, laugh of puzzlement.

"You mean you don't know how old you are?! It's time for you to start keeping track of these things!"

What does she think? She thinks, "He says I need to know how old I am. I have to start keeping track of such things."

What things? The calendar, of course.

"I have to start keeping track of the calendar."

What is this all about?

It's about girls learning to keep track of the calendar, the days of the month. It's the beginning of sex education, without a single word being said about sex.

No embarrassment at all. We're only talking about how old she is. That's Parallel Accessing. That's Indirection.

How to Live to Be a Hundred.

One of the more futile things in this world is trying to give good advice to teenagers. But if you know how to do Parallel Accessing you can sometimes achieve surprising results.

With kids approaching the age of sixteen, I sometimes begin the annual checkup by telling them we no longer think in terms of a lifespan of seventy-some years. More and more people are living into their eighties, nineties, even a hundred or more. Some people are living a hundred and ten or even a hundred and twenty years.

I say, "Now you may think, 'What's that got to do with me, I'm not even sixteen,' but if you want to live a really long life, you have to avoid getting knocked off before your time. You have to know, the thing that will kill you when you're sixteen, seventeen, all the way up to twenty-six, is the automobile. From sixteen to twenty-six, the thing that will kill you is the automobile. So when you get that driver's license at sixteen, you make sure you are the one in that driver's seat. Nobody else gets to drive you unless they are as old as your parents. Because you know your parents know how to drive and you know that you know how to drive, but you don't know how good a driver that other kid is. You know you care about staying alive, but you don't know about the other kid.

"This means, of course, that you're going to have to have your own car!"

"Now, from twenty-six to sixty, the thing that will kill you is cigarettes. Lung cancer. You smoke, you will die before you're sixty. And it's really hard to stop, so don't start.

"Now, after sixty, from sixty on to eighty, ninety, a hundred and ten, that's the tricky part. If you want to live a long and happy life, you have to stay on good terms with your Mom and Dad. You're stuck with them, so you may as well start practicing now."

I'm not handing them a set of rules. They've heard so many rules they're sick of rules. I'm just telling them how to live a hundred and ten years.

Teeth

With many little boys, the first word they learn after "mama" and "dada" is "Pterodactyl", or "Tyrannosaurus rex." They have a secret desire to grow up and become a Palaeontologist. It's those big teeth. That's what gets 'em. So you talk to them about their big sharp teeth and you ask them to show you their big sharp teeth. They never heard of tonsils, you don't ask them to show you their tonsils. And you don't ask them to open their mouth, you ask to see their big sharp teeth. And they will gladly show you their big sharp teeth and they will even growl for you like a Tyrannosaurus.

You're talking to them about dinosaur teeth and they are translating it into their own potency, their own powers of aggression, which at this age have need of expression and far too little opportunity. And they are grateful to you for the opportunity to show a little guilt-free aggression, to be a little aggressive and get praised for it.

That's Parallel Accessing. It's also Pacing. And it's Reframing the mouth examination into an interest in big sharp teeth.

Talking about your own experiences causes others to access their own similar experiences. I wish I could get across to you how powerful this effect is and how silently it operates. When people talk, they usually are just talking about what spontaneously occurs to them and they don't usually take stock of the effect their words might be having on someone else, such as their spouse or their child. Plan your speech. Think about the effect you want to produce.

"When you get to grad school we'll deal with that."

You say that when they're in the seventh grade. You don't say another word, and it will sink down into their unconscious. They're going to be the person to go to grad school. How can they argue against it? How can they build any defenses against it? You've just taken it for granted. And you get that long-term effect. They may decide not to go after all. But they have thought about it.

The same thing is true of behavior. We use the body language that expresses our emotional state without considering the effect it may have on someone else. It's when you bring your speech and your body language into the service of producing a desired effect—that's when you become a Strategic Parent.

If you start to talk about your own childhood, pretty soon anyone listening to you will be remembering things from their own childhood. You don't even have to talk about the subject that you want to discuss, you can talk about something parallel and produce an experience.

Words have this incredible power to call up experience. So you can understand that when you say a word to your child, you conjure up as if by magic a whole world of their own experience. This is one of the ways by which you can get into another person's world. This is not a voluntary choice on your child's part. There is no way that they can refuse to experience those associations, because those associations are what that word means to them.

And you understand what a momentous thing you are doing when you speak words to your child or your spouse or to any other person. You have the power to create their experience, you have the power to shape it, to make it beautiful. You can give them the experience of competence, of comfort, of success.

5.

BODY LOGIC

The kids are in the bathroom, brushing their teeth, and you start the bedtime story while they are still brushing their teeth. Next day they start brushing their teeth a little earlier. What has happened? Their body tells them that brushing their teeth makes the bedtime story begin. They want that bedtime story, so they start brushing their teeth. That's conditioning, or Body Logic. If they are seven or eight years old, they know with their brain that tooth-brushing doesn't cause bedtime stories to begin, but their body knows otherwise, because it has experienced otherwise. By linking two events together in time, you have caused them to be linked togther in your children's nervous system.

This is not a voluntary thing. They may decide they don't want the bedtime story, they may decide not to brush their teeth, but they can't decide not to feel that connection, because it's in their body, not their brain. One of the nurses in our office saw her thirteen-year-old daughter fondling the tattered blanket she has had since the age of two. She asked, "What does your blanket smell like, Tammy?"

And Tammy replied, "Safe things!"

The body remembers. The body never forgets.

There's a Dad in our practice who always wears Mom's bathrobe when he gets up at night to take care of the baby, because then the baby can smell Mom and feel safe.

It's in your power as parents to create these linkages. You make a link between a powerful source of satisfaction and the performance of a certain behavioral sequence. You don't say anything. You don't want them to analyze it away. You can transform their entire life, almost, and your own, too, into experiences of deep satisfaction linked to the performance of everyday tasks.

The Now and Then Tooth Fairy

Kyle has a very special tooth fairy. She leaves a quarter under the pillow when he sheds a tooth, but recently she has started leaving a quarter under his pillow at irregular intervals, every week or so. When Kyle asked his mother why this was happening, she had no idea.

"Maybe it's just because you were extra good."

Kyle spends whole weeks being extra good because the tooth fairy might come again.

The technical name for this is Intermittent Reinforcement, but it works even if you don't know the name of it.

6.

BREAKING IT UP

The Magic Door

If you have ever taken your baby to the doctor's office for shots you may have noticed that if the baby cries, they will often instantly stop as Mother carries them out through the door frame. It's like just turning off a switch.

That's that tendency, that we all have, to compartmentalize. When we shift locations, we often shift our ego state. When you're in a different ego state, it's real hard to remember what it felt like in the other ego state. You know how it is. When you feel good, you wonder, "How could I have been so depressed the other night, I can't even remember." Or when you're depressed, "How could I ever feel good again?" That's this shifting of ego states, and of course the whole art that we're talking about is based upon shifting ego states. When you go from one ego state to the next, your previous, locked-in pattern of behavior is all interrupted. You can't remember what was happening in the previous one—you usually don't even notice how the shift came about.

Get Them Started On Something Else.

Simply going through a door or moving the action to a different room will often induce a change. The dining room may be the location where all the bad stuff takes place, where the fights go on, but when the kids are in the bedroom or in the playroom, it's totally different. You just invite a shift of ego state by the simple maneuver of moving the whole scene somewhere else, like having a picnic in the bedroom. Or you can change something to make the old scene into a new experience—like having blue macaroni for lunch.

Going through a doorway is something that's pretty concrete, but you can shift your body position and cause a shift in the ego states of the people around you. If you're leaning forward, frowning, with your finger wagging at the kid, what can you expect? Defiance! Or cowering. Fight or flight. Primitive, default-type reactions.

But if you lean back, relax your posture, and throw 'em a blanket, or the car keys, you will trigger a switch of ego states and you'll be in a whole different scene and dealing with a different problem from the one that you had before. Hopefully it will be a better one!

The idea is, if you don't want a certain piece of behavior to take place, initiate a piece of behavior that is incompatible.

Nonevents Selective Blindness)

(You can carry this all the way to where something is a nonevent, where you don't put any name at all on it. It's the strategy called Selective Blindness. If the parent does not notice that the toddler has fallen down, but goes on talking as if nothing had happened, the kid—you can see this for yourself—they will sit there with this puzzled look on their face. They will look at mom and dad. They will look for that shocked expression that tells them something awful has happened and they should cry. Sometimes they'll start to cry and then stop because Mom and Dad don't even seem to notice. You can make something into a nonevent. This is a very powerful technique. You want to be careful to use it prudently.

Give Them a Friendly Divorce

Sibling Rivalry—the green-eyed monster—is one of those problems that parents struggle with. And the more idealistic they are, the less able they are to cope with it. It's appalling to see their lovely toddler going for the baby with murder in his eye. Mom rescues the baby and the toddler starts breaking up the furniture or torturing Mom with whining and demanding. What's to be done? The books aren't much help. The books talk about how nice it is to have quality time together and how wonderful family togetherness is. They even want the offending sibling to hang around and watch Mom breastfeeding the baby. Older brother watches, then wants his turn at the breast. Mom lectures him about how he is supposed to enjoy this togetherness and he just behaves worse.

What the toddler needs in this situation is a friendly divorce. Don't make him watch the baby being breastfed unless he really does put a positive spin on it. Don't make him hang around while Mommy is caring for the baby. Give him a separate life, a separate career. Let him get started on activities out of the house. Let him come in to see the baby for a few seconds once or twice a day. Make it a rare privilege to see the baby.

It really is true that in some circumstances absence makes the heart grow fonder.

7.

TOYING WITH THE REALITY

The Real Meaning of a Colicky Baby.

When parents get their first or their second or third baby home from the hospital, they often don't have the faintest idea about colic. When their lovely baby, only two or three weeks old, begins to scream and shriek and turn purple for six hours at a time, they bring him to the doctor because they are afraid something terrible is wrong. And when they learn that it's not a disease but it's still incurable and they are going to have to put up with it for thirteen more weeks, they're not exactly overjoyed.

I tell them their baby has been born with extra pizzazz in his nervous system. He's going to be very noisy for thirteen weeks and then he's going to be the nicest baby they ever could wish for. And when he starts going to school he's probably going to do his homework, because he has extra pizzazz in his nervous system. And if he likes school, he'll probably go on to get his Ph.D., because he has that extra intellectual drive. Or maybe he'll turn out to be a musician or an artist or a writer, or a downhill skier. Whatever he picks, he'll do it with that extra drive and succeed at it. And when he is an adult, he'll send you that check in the mail every month to reward you for all those years of supporting him.

A colicky baby is money in the bank. Think of that whenever he screeches and keeps you awake at night.

I'm not talking about a noisy baby. I'm talking about extra pizzazz, about scholarship, about future success, and money in the bank.

That's the Strategy called Reframing. It's also Parallel Accessing and Future Pacing. (These strategies overlap and blend into each other. In real life you can't ever do just one thing. There are always overtones.)

What Does It Mean To Them? (The Meaning of a Communication)

There's a delightful little book that I hope all of you will some day read and enjoy. It has a rather strange title. It's called *Appropriate Technology* and the subtitle is: *Technology with a Human Face*. In that book Professor Dunn, the author, tells a marvelous story about the African tsetse fly that carries sleeping sickness. It seems that a certain lecturer on health matters always carried with him a large eighteen inch model of the tsetse fly for purposes of illustration. After one such lecture, a member of the audience came up to him and said that he could understand how such flies could be a health menace, but fortunately, the local variety were a good deal smaller. They weren't anywhere near eighteen inches long.

Professor Dunn says that experience taught him that although every picture tells a story, the story it tells may not be the same for everyone. The meaning of a communication is what the other person makes of it, and that's not necessarily the same as what you intended. It's up to you to notice that. That's your feedback.

Changing The Metaphor

Professor Dunn goes on to tell another story, this one about a public health team, working in Ethiopia during a time of drought. They drilled a borehole to supply safe drinking water for a small village, but to their dismay some person or persons unknown kept filling it up with rocks at night. Finally they realized that the local water carriers, who used to bring in drinking water in animal skins on the backs of donkeys from a distant water hole—those men had been put out of a job and had no livelihood. The team appointed them as guardians of the new borehole at a good salary and the vandalism immediately ceased.

In the old frame of reference, the men had been vandals. In the new frame, they were policemen—and they never needed a single day's worth of rehabilitation.

Praise the Explorer

If you can learn to do smooth shifts of frame of reference, you can sometimes achieve incredible results. When the toddler starts getting into the pots and pans in the kitchen, you can say, "Wow! You really like to be an explorer, don't you?" But maybe you are noticing that it's you, the parent, who has to do the first frame shift. You have to shift your own frame of reference about what the child is doing. You have to drop the old frame of reference that the child is misbehaving or being a nuisance or whatever your old response was and realize for yourself, "Oh, of course! This is a young scientist just getting started on a wonderful career of exploring the whole world! I need to encourage this kind of behavior, not try to eliminate it." Once you've shifted your own frame, you'll find it very easy and even spontaneous to use the right strategies.

When a little kid grabs something, at two years or three years of age, and you redefine it as "stealing", what have you done? You've turned a spontaneous behavior into a sin. I don't think that's very useful.

Or if a four-year-old tells you about the monster under the bed and you redefine it as "lying", what you've done is to create a character defect. You've done it by your choice of words.

But if a kid falls down, and looks up at you startled, you can say, "Ka-boom!" with that upward lilt in your voice and a bit of a smile. It's OK to fall down a few times when you're learning to walk. It's OK to make a few mistakes in a good cause.

If they are a little older, you can say, "A-ha! studying gravity again, eh?"

You've redefined the situation in a really constructive way.

This is a technique that's very useful, but it also has some pitfalls because redefining a situation involves toying with the reality. If you're going to do it, you need to know what you're doing.

The power to put a name on something is the power to make it a destructive negative experience, or the power to make it a positive experience. Remember John Milton? Paradise Lost? "The mind is its own place and in itself, can make a heaven of hell, a hell of heaven?" When you call something by a really powerful name, you have had a powerful influence on the other person. If a kid at age three or four is told that what he does is stealing and lying, he may end up struggling, all his life to deal with stealing and lying. But if you use a constructive term for it, they may understand that they have this wonderful spontaneous impulse to explore the world, and to pick things up and look at them and study them. All they need to do is to learn that it's socially acceptable to give it back after they've studied it. You don't even use the word "stealing" at all. You don't use the word "lying" when you talk about monsters. You say, "What a great story you told." Or you get very interested in the monster. You let him tell you all about it.

The Value Of Money

Three year old Justin likes to fish in Daddy's pockets and take out the change. He gives it to Mom to give to the people at work. Mom was trying to teach him, "It's not so cool to take money from other people—it's noble to want to give it to people who don't have as much, but what's in Daddy's wallet needs to stay in Daddy's wallet." Justin listened to his Mom's words, but it was just too much for a three-year-old to absorb.

It's easy to redefine this situation.

"Oh, wow! I see you're really interested in coins!"

"You're really interested in exploring things!"

"You really like to find stuff in wallets!"

Or you get him a wallet of his own.

You can redefine almost anything so that it will tend in a constructive direction, but you have to have some skill in redefining. You have to practice it.

Why Not Learn To Fly The Real Thing?

Our son Dave had been an avid model airplane enthusiast ever since the age of seven. When he got to be fourteen, he said, "I want a motorcycle." He had already taken a used car apart and left it in the backyard.

We were thinking, "Oh, my God. Another motorcycle bum."

Then my wife did this amazing thing, just on the spur of the moment. She said, "What do you want to mess around with motorcycles for? You've been a model airplane builder all your life. Why don't you learn to fly the real thing?"

She said, "I'll take you down to Willow Run and we'll do a trial flight today, right now."

She drove this fourteen year old out to Willow Run on the spur of the moment, located the pilot and said, "My son wants to fly!"

She sat out on the tarmac and watched.

Half an hour went by, the time was up for the five dollars, forty-five minutes, fifty minutes, an hour—and she began to wonder, where did they go? Did they crash?

Then the plane appeared and began to wobble back towards the airport and wobblingly circled the airport and wobblingly came down and bounced a little bit and came to a stop and—out jumped Dave!

"Mom, I flew it! I flew it!"

There never was any talk again about motorcycles. He was going to be an airplane pilot.

Only One Left

Cheryl has kids who hate fruit and won't eat it. She has solved this problem by bringing out one apple or one banana and saying, "Oh, I only have one of these. I guess I'll just have to give it to Anna."

Sarah immediately demands to have one also. Cheryl ends up by dividing the item in two and giving each child an equal share.

You could think of it as Reframing the eating of fruit into a question of Equal Rights for rival siblings.

Pre-emptive Frame-Setting.

This is a really big one. It means forestalling problems by setting the right tone at the beginning. So much of our human interactions are reactive to the other person, we often don't even realize the other person is setting the pace or controlling the tone. Pre-emptive frame-setting means moving right in and establishing a pace and a tone and even a specific orientation right from the beginning. Being human, we tend to go along rather than make the effort to change what's already started.

But there is a caution! You have to be believable if you want to do Pre-emptive Frame-setting. So you start with the basic rule of Pacing with the other person even as you set the frame.

To set the frame with a two year old or a three or four year old you look surprised and say, "What's that on your shoe?!!"

They will stop in their tracks, look down, and carefully examine their shoe.

Or you say, "What's that on your shirt?" and they will stop and look down to study their shirt. And they may look up again and say, "New boots!" or "Turtles on my shirt!" or whatever.

You don't know just what they will say, but you are prepared to answer them back again, and you are very, very interested in this topic of such interest to them. You become a co-investigator with the child of this topic of such absorbing interest to them.

And with a little girl, you are very interested in earrings.

"Do you wear earrings?"

"Does Mommy let you wear clip-ons?"

"Do you like pink or blue ones better?"

"Do you put pink paint on your fingernails? Does Mommy let you do that? And what colors do you like best? Does Mommy let you use the little paintbrush?"

"And do you paint your toenails, too?"

Where you go from there is up to you. You have set the frame for your interaction with the child and it is something of great interest to the child.

The First Tool

Parents sometimes come to me in a state of anxiety because someone has told them they must break their child's Pacifier Habit. They've been told of the dire consequences of the Pacifier Habit. They've tried to take it away but their child objects loudly. He seems to be addicted to his pacifier. He's in love with It. I point out to them that Man is the tool-using creature par excellence. It's our necessary fate as well as one of our deepest satisfactions to learn to use tools of every sort to achieve our goals. The pacifier is the very first tool we learn to use.

"You don't want to mess that up."

Of course they don't want to mess up their child's tool-using abilities. They want their child to grow up to be able to use pen and pencil, to type on the keyboard, to throw a ball, to reassemble a carburetor.

The pacifier is suddenly something very important—to keep.

8.

TOGGLE SWITCHES

A little kid, maybe two or three years old, came into the office, and after a few seconds he realized that he could jump up on the chair and get to the light switch. He was having fun, flipping the lights on and off. I sidled over and said, "Oh, I see you like to do the light switch!" and he goes, "Yeah," with this great grin on his face. I said, "And you like to turn it on!"

"Yeah!"

"And you like to turn it off!"

"Yeah!"

"Oh, OK, turn it on!"

So he turned it on.

I said, "Turn it off!"

He turned it off. I said, "Turn it on!"

He turned it on. I said, "Turn it off, on, off, on, off, on, off."

After about a minute of this he looked at me and said, "Ecchh!"

He realized that I had hooked him and he jumped down and ran out of the room, laughing.

John Gall, MD, FAAP

He Didn't Want His Ears Examined

I saw a little kid who absolutely did not want to have his ears looked at. It was clear that he was bound and determined to resist me no matter what I did. It was clear that he was going to get a great deal of satisfaction out of resisting me. So, I decided that I would give him an opportunity to resist me, systematically.

As he was sitting there in the chair next to his mom, I said, "Open your eyes," so he started to close his eyes; but he didn't really want to close his eyes, what he wanted to do was to resist me. He was breathing fairly regularly, so as he took another breath, I said, "Now close your eyes." I had just said, "Open your eyes," and they had sort of sagged. I said, "Close your eyes," and he triumphantly raised them wide open. Then I said, "Open your eyes," and they really did close. Then I said, "Close your eyes," and he opened them. Then I said, "Open your eyes," and he closed them. His breathing began to get very regular and deep, and I said, "Open your eyes, close your eyes," and he was very, very satisfied with himself because he was absolutely doing the opposite of what I wanted. Every time I said, "Close your eyes," he opened his eyes, and when I said, "Open your eyes," he closed his eyes.

He was so satisfied that his head gradually fell down on his chest and he began to snore, opening and closing his eyes as I continued to instruct him to close and open his eyes. As he did that, I put one hand against one ear and looked in the other ear, and I continued to tell him to open and close his eyes. He was so busy resisting me that there was just no resistance left over for the ear exam.

I got more compliance than I had bargained for! He actually went into a trance. You really don't need that much effect for ordinary everyday parenting!

But he was satisfied, he was resisting me, and I was perfectly happy to have him resist me. He didn't realize that he was doing exactly what I was commanding, he was just one half-wave off, you might say. He just had the toggle switches reversed. So we were all very happy with that arrangement.

Compliance, resistance, this is the magic key. If your child is resisting you, if you're aware of that fact, you use the strategies that build upon the polarity.

Too Little To Do "X"

A kid of three to four years is coming into the examining room, and as he glances around I say to him, "You're too little to get up on my table—"and he says, "Oh, no I'm not!!!"

"Well, you may be able to get on my table, but you sure can't reach that mobile up there."

The next thing you know, he's standing on the table, he's reaching up to pull on the mobile. I examine his liver and spleen, he doesn't even notice. He's doing what he wants to do, I'm doing what I want to do. We're both winning.

He isn't being frustrated. He's being allowed to do what he wants to do, and the thing that he wants to do most of all at that moment is to prove that I'm wrong. So I let him prove that I'm wrong.

You Let Them Win Once In A While

Then I say: "Wow! You really can!" and he says, "Yeah! I'm big!"

"I'm separate from you." That's the assertion of autonomy. That's the way it works, and that's how you foster it. You give them a chance to beat you. You give them a chance to win.

Squinching Down (Let Them Be Bigger)

Little kids dream of being big, of being even bigger than the grownups. You can actually convey that to them just by squinching down, so that they look down on you. That act alone conveys everything that needs to be said.

Tippy-toes

One of my patients, a little girl, two years old, was wearing brand-new shiny black patent-leather shoes. I squatted down to her level and said, "You've got shiny new shoes!" And she beamed.

Then I asked, "Can you stand on your tippy-toes?"

She beamed. In her shiny new shoes, she could do that. To her, it wasn't part of the neurological assessment. It was a moment of warm satisfaction, a moment to savor her own undeniable worthwhileness and competence.

Restraining A Change (Building Anticipation)

This is a strategy you can use when you really want them to do something. You use expressions like, "Well, you're really not quite old enough for that."

"You're not big enough to take a bath and wash yourself all by yourself."

"You're not big enough to buckle teddy bear up, are you?"

Then you let them surprise you.

"What a big boy you are, you surprised me."

The Extended Tom Sawyer Maneuver

Now, if Dad is always going off to his room to play with his Macintosh computer—gee, that must be fun, because the adults are into it. That's the Tom Sawyer Maneuver.

How Not to Examine a Baby

I've seen a professor examining a newborn baby to show a student how to do it. The baby is lying on the table, waving his arms and legs, looking around, opening and closing his eyes, opening and closing his mouth, yawning, sneezing, doing everything. Then here comes the professor! He wants to look in the baby's mouth. He takes a tongue blade and puts it in the baby's mouth, and the baby promptly clamps his jaws together, so the professor has to force the baby's jaws open to look in the mouth.

Then the professor wants to look in the baby's eyes with his light, so he takes this real bright light and he shines it right into the baby's eyes and baby clamps his eyes shut. Then the professor has to take his fingers and pry those little eyelids open.

You can get a baby's eyes to open spontaneously by turning off the lights. You don't have to pry their eyes open.

Every mother knows how to get a baby to open their mouth. One mother in our practice knows that her baby likes to suck on his own big toe, so she puts his big toe up there and he opens his mouth.

There are so many different ways to do anything. You're only limited by what you can think of.

The professor wanted to look at the baby's palms, so he pulled on the baby's fingers. What happens when you do that? The baby makes a fist. Then you have to pry the fingers open to see what's going on.

You can touch the back of a baby's hand and their hand will open.

In every case the doctor was producing the defensive reaction that made his task difficult. He was not utilizing the feedback that he was getting from the baby, to be a signal to modify his own behavior. The baby was yawning, but the doctor was examining the feet. The baby's mouth was open, but the doctor was examining the feet! Now it's obvious that somewhere between the first week of life and age forty or fifty, something rather serious happens. We stop using our feedback.

We're carefully taught to pay attention to the program inside our head, instead of what's happening in the real world.

It just doesn't make sense to trigger resistances unnecessarily.

9.

LOSING YOUR MARBLES

You start out, when they are babies, by being 100% competent in caring for them. As they grow, you begin to lose some skills. By the time they are in seventh grade, you have forgotten how to do algebra. They can't even count on you to remember to wake them up for school.

Powerful Katrina

Now Katrina was eight years old and her IQ was over 140 but she could not get out of bed in the mornings in time to catch the school bus. Mornings were a terrible hassle. Mom had to rouse her up out of bed, argue with her about which clothes to wear and then actually dress her, comb her hair and fix breakfast, nag her to move faster, and then as the school bus approached, she had to shove Katrina out the front door. On many mornings Katrina was just too late, the school bus drove on by and Mom had to drive her to school. And Katrina's IQ was over 140.

Now you can bet they had had plenty of heart-to-heart talks and Katrina agreed that it was unfair that Mom had to do everything for a big strong girl with an IQ over 140, but things didn't get any better. Mom was getting madder and madder. So she came to see us.

The Flaky Moms And Dads Club

We suggested that Katrina was not getting the opportunity to use that IQ and that resourcefulness in constructive ways to meet her own needs because Mom was too competent. Mom was extremely competent in waking up on time, in rousing Katrina up out of bed, in making breakfast, in combing Katrina's hair, in running outdoors to stop the school bus, in driving Katrina to school. We suggested that Mom very quietly and very gradually begin to lose her marbles, to forget to set the alarm clock, to oversleep, to put too much salt in the eggs and burn the toast.

She could lose her skill at combing Katrina's hair, she could forget to do the laundry when Katrina's clean clothes were used up. She could forget to put gas in the car. She could remain the same loving Mom, ever willing to help, but her help would be the kind of help people can gladly do without, the kind you regret ever asking for. In a word, we invited Mom to join our secret society, the Flaky Moms and Dads Club.

In less than two weeks Katrina decided that her scalp would be healthier if she combed her own hair, her breakfast would taste better if she made it herself, and she would be more likely to catch the bus and get to school if she set her own alarm clock and got up by herself. Strangest of all, as her fights with Mom became a thing of the past, she found herself admiring and respecting and loving her Flaky old Mom more and more. Katrina is in her teens now and she and her Mom are good friends.

Katrina's problem fundamentally was that she needed to move on to the next higher stage of her development, that stage where she would begin to take responsibility for some of her own behavior. The technical tactic of using the Flaky Moms' and Dads' club strategy works when the problem is one of moving to the next higher level of responsibility. It would not necessarily be appropriate in some other context.

Using Your Weakness

When a parent says, "I wish you would do your homework," the child is all ready to resist, but they have to agree that it is true that you as the parent do wish that they would do their homework. They have to agree with you about that.

Then when you also say, "But I know I can't make you," they have to agree with you about that. They've agreed with you twice inside of one second. You have forced them to agree with you—twice.

Both parts of that sentence are absolutely, compellingly true. The child has to say, "Yes" twice in a row. "I wish you would do your homework." The child says, "She wishes I would do my homework. I know that's true." Then you say, "But I can't make you." She'll say, "That's right. You can't make me." She knows that. That sentence is about all you will ever want to say about homework. Use it sparingly. Say it once a year. That's all it takes.

It's amazing how fast kids learn. The child agrees that it's true, the parent agrees that it's true, they all understand that this is true. So, if there's going to be something happening around homework, it's going to be based on this real truth, that parents cannot make you do it. Which is the truth!

The thing to avoid is the attempt to be powerful and authoritative and fail.So don't ask them to do what you cannot enforce. In the case of teenagers who are very independent spirited, you say, "I wish you would do your homework, but of course I can't make you."

Night Lights

Two-and-a-half year old Brett was fascinated by lights. He spent a lot of time going around turning them on and off, pulling out the plugs and pushing them in again His parents bought him some night lights for his own room and stood right there and supervised him while he plugged them in.

"Oh light! Neat!"

Now he leaves the lights alone all day, but every evening he summons his parents.

"We have to go around and turn off all the lights!"

That is his contribution to the family. He's the night watchman!

Self-Service

At mealtimes one family has the kids pass the bowls around and serve themselves. They use paper plates with three or four sections in the plate. The kids dole out enough carrots to fit into one section and that's enough carrots. When the next bowl comes around they put the next item in the next little compartment.

It's amazing how much food those kids put away. They ask for second and third servings of food. No fuss, no discussion, just, "Pass the peas, please!"

You can get a lot of mileage out of Putting the Kids in Charge.

The Magic Phrase, "I wonder if…"

You tell your fourteen-year-old, "I'm so absent-minded. I left the car in the driveway. I wonder if you could drive it into the garage for me?"

Memorize that phrase, "I wonder if…" It's really powerful.

Death-Toy

Our older son wanted to fly hanggliders. This was back in the days when they didn't have stabilizers, and they were falling out of the sky. We bit our lips hard and kept quiet. Time went by, our son fell in love. He brought his sweetheart home to meet us. We heard them in the garage.

"What's that thing up there, hanging from the ceiling?"

"Oh, that's my hangglider!" Spoken with pride.

Long silence.

"Death-toy! Either it goes or I go!"

That was the end of it. It rotted in place.

Later they got married.

If your own voice is too weak, try letting them hear it from someone with a stronger voice.

You don't tell a young hero what he can't do.

10.

PLAYING BOTH SIDES

When you speak to someone, they split into two pieces. This happens all the time, to everybody. There is a part that wants to go along with what you say, and then there's a part that wants to defend their individuality, they're not going along. There's a part that agrees, and a part that disagrees, simultaneously. Nobody is ever 100% compliant or 100% resistant.

So your job is to keep your eyes and ears open and notice whether your child's compliance is stronger or their resistance is stronger, because if the resistance is stronger, you can then jump over to the other side and let them resist you and succeed in resisting you and thus do the thing that you want. That way, you both win.

"Of course you want to be a baby and pee your pants. Here, let's get out your old diapers again." There's always a part that's conservative and wants to go back to the good old ways. Talk to that part, validate it!

The Yin And The Yang

I remember something David Brinkley once said a long time ago on TV. He was talking about his family and he said, "Togetherness is great, but don't knock getawayness!"

That's part of the Yin and Yang, too. The kids need you to be there and they also need you to be away. They need you to be firm and authoritarian, they need you to be flaky and absent. In other words they need both sides of every equation.

Mom and Dad can take opposite sides of an issue. Mom can say a three-year-old is big enough to drink his milk, and Dad can say, "No, he's too little." Whichever course the child chooses, he's going along with one of his parents and resisting the other one. Either way, he gets to win. It's not the milk that's important here. It's the interaction.

Both of Mom's kids were sitting on the floor, crying to be helped. Mom sat on the floor with them and started crying, too. They both stopped and looked at Mom as if to say, "Don't be silly!"

Encouraging A Regression (The Good Old Ways).

A kid will move forward real fast, and they will scare themselves, and they will need to have a regression. That's where the savvy parent will encourage them to regress. No matter what it is, bed wetting or anything at all. You will encourage them to regress because that leaves the door open. They're moving forward so fast they scare themselves. They're moving away from babyhood at rocket speed, and they look back and they say, "Oh, oh! I'll never be able to be a baby again. I need to be a baby for a while." You let them regress. It's the yin and yang. You have the advance, you have the fallback and then the advance again. It's a very wise parent who will allow that and even encourage it.

So you Encourage a Regression. "Of course you want to be a baby! Here, let's get out your old blanket."

A new baby can cause the older child to oscillate between advancing and regressing.

"You want to be a baby but you don't want to have diapers on. We'll just put 'em in the bureau here by your bed."

He can say, "No, No, No! I don't want 'em in my room!"

"Oh, you don't want them in your room. Where would you like them to be?" No matter what he does, he's stuck with the darn diapers, because he's regressing and you are helping him.

"Well, why don't we just keep them nearby just in case you change your mind. It would be a good thing to have them around." You could ask him if he would like that. Then he could say yes or he could say no. You keep the options open. You keep your own options open, and you keep his options open, until finally he works himself into a situation that is satisfactory to you both.

On the Potty, With a Diaper

Megan was happy enough to poop in her diaper, but she was afraid to sit on the toilet. When Mother spread a diaper over the toilet, Megan was happy to poop in her diaper on the toilet. Later she was happy to dispense with the diaper and just sit on the toilet to poop.

Orientation Every Day

Michael was fine the first day he went to day care, which was orientation day, but he cried constantly the entire time for the second, third, and fourth days. Mom met with the daycare staff and they agreed to let Michael go to "orientation" every day (that is, to let Mom stay in the same room with him for the entire session). After a week Michael was happy to stay without Mom present.

Regression is as much a part of that process of moving ahead as the concavity of the wave is, that makes the next wave. You have to have it. If you know that, you can encourage it. Then the kid says, "Ahhh! I can still be a baby! But wait a minute, I'd rather be grown up." So he moves ahead again. You help him move back and then you help him move forward again. He's happy, he feels comfortable. And you feel comfortable!

11.

PLOPPING ON THEIR PERCH

Wrinkly Chicken

Susanna and Leora, who were just two years apart in age, worked as a team to frustrate Mom. They just didn't like the way their food was served at mealtime. They wouldn't eat their sandwich because it wasn't cut just exactly in the middle. They wouldn't drink their juice because the two glasses weren't just exactly equally full. They even refused delicious fried chicken because the skin was all wrinkly.

To Mom's consternation, I agreed with the girls that they really ought not to eat such food. I suggested to Mom that she continue to prepare it as she always had done, but at the last moment of offering it she was to jerk it back and discover the flaw for herself: "Oh! I'm sorry, this sandwich isn't cut right. You won't want this. I'm going to throw it away."

"Oh! I'm sorry, this chicken is all wrinkly. You don't want this. I'll put it away."

And what happened? The girls cried out together, "I'll eat it, I'll eat it."

And that was the end of that problem.

Family Career Slots

What happened there? Very simple. The function of criticizing and refusing food had been taken over by Mom, so the kids were free to flop down on the other perch, the career slot of being really hungry and let's not nitpick about good food.

So when a child repeatedly exhibits behavior you'd rather they didn't, consider that they may be stuck in an unfortunate family career slot. You can help them out of it by quietly moving in and taking over that slot for yourself. Later on, if you wish, you can find another career for yourself.

Plopping On Their Perch.

You move in and take over the child's Family Career Slot. Once you've made it Mom's Thing many kids won't have anything to do with it.

You've no doubt read how parents ought to show an interest in their child's activities and be a pal to their kids and of course there's a lot of truth in that, but how many kids have been turned off to a hobby or an interesting line of activity because their parents got too much into it.

Remember our twenty-one-monther who kept insisting, "No help Luke!" He didn't want it to be Mom's thing, he wanted it to be his thing.

Taking Possession Of The Symptom By Making It Mom's Or Dad's Thing

If there's anything a kid is ambivalent about, it's to realize that they have been captured into Mom's system and they're doing what Mom wants—or Dad. So that gives you the power. You now have created a situation where if they're going to resist you, they have to stop doing it.

On the other hand, if they want to go along with you, you know how to handle that. You just keep encouraging them.

This is where you actually ally yourself with the resistant behavior, and from that position you have the power to go this way or that way. You can go yea or nay, you can play the compliance or the resistance and it's your choice, which means that you have that wonderful feeling of being in control of the situation.

Dolphins That Have Tantrums

Karen Pryor, the famous animal trainer, developed a series of strategies for dealing with animals. Eventually she became a trainer of animal trainers.

One of the things that she mentions in her book entitled *Don't Shoot The Dog* is that the moment *before* you have learned something new is a moment of extreme frustration. She has seen this repeatedly with dolphins. They just have a tantrum, literally leaping out of the water, splashing their whole body, throwing water all around, getting the trainer wet, and then it dawns on them, "Oh! That's what's wanted. That's what I'm supposed to do."

In that moment they have moved up one step. They have gone from a stage of not knowing to a stage of knowing, they have gone from not knowing how to do this particular performance up to the level of knowing how to do it. This is true for kids too. If you see a kid being really frustrated in their homework or something like that, just tell yourself, "That's the learning tantrum, the Prelearning Dip."

The only way that you can really learn something new is to accept the fact that part of the old can't be true any more.

And that's real rough especially for little children who are learning something new every day.

Having A Comfortable Tantrum (Making It Mom's Thing)

A tantrum is a legitimate piece of behavior for a little kid. A tantrum is a very straight expression of their frustration. But you can point out that they haven't got it down quite right, they need a little more practice. They could pound a little more with their fists, yell a little louder. In fact, maybe it would be a good idea to have a little regular tantrum practice two or three times a day.

Some of their tantrums are probably a part of learning and if you look at them positively that way, your response will be quite different. Instead of saying, "Don't be such a stinker, don't lie there screaming and crying," you can say, "Oh, you're having a tantrum, aren't you? Are you really comfortable there on the floor? Can I get you anything?"

"Would you like a pillow to kick against instead?"

"When you're finished we can have some milk and cookies together. But be sure you're really finished!"

The Perils Of Dawdling (Hidden Symmetry)

Now with dawdling, you can be the one who holds them up, without saying a word about it. You can be the one that just can't quite get everything ready. You insert a Hidden Symmetry into the situation, what Milton Erickson called the absolute peril of dawdling. You don't have to say anything.

If Mom and Dad have a behavior pattern that involves the kid wanting to get somewhere, or to get something done in a hurry, and Mom and Dad are struggling and hurrying and delaying, that'll be a pattern that the kid hates. They may hate it in themselves, particularly if they do it more and discover that Mom and Dad get worse. Kids try to psych out the way the universe works. They try to psych out cause and effect. At some unconscious level they may actually believe

71

that because they're dawdling more, Mom and Dad are dawdling more. It's that Body Logic thing.

12.

SHAKING THE FOUNDATIONS

A child's security is based upon the certainty and the faith that their parents are firm and unwavering in their dedication to each other, to civilized behavior, reasonableness, etc. The idea that their parents might freak out, disappear, or split from each other is hard for a child to handle.

There's a situation in the doctor's office where the little kid has taken off his shoes and socks and he's finished with the exam and he's gotten quite comfortable and now he doesn't want to go home. He doesn't want to put his shoes and socks on.

At that point sometimes I will suggest, "Why don't you just leave your shoes and socks off because you don't have to go home with Mom and Dad. Let them go home by themselves."

I say, "Mom and Dad can leave, you can stay here. You don't want to put your shoes and socks on and go with Mom and Dad."

This shakes the foundations of their security. To be away from home and threatened with separation from their parents is scary. I've threatened their security.

Stretching The Little Old Umbilical Cord.

There is an invisible umbilical cord that connects the kid to the parents. Toddlers like to dart away. They'll even get out of sight. They could be kidnapped. You say, "Come back, come back!"and they laugh. Then you scold them for not coming back, and you argue with them about it. They have not come to the end of their umbilical cord yet. So what you do is, you give them the opportunity to find out where the end of the umbilical cord is.

Leaving The Scene

In the supermarket, you can go around the aisles and keep track of them and know where they are. There will be a period of time when they don't realize that they've lost contact but then they will realize that they have lost contact. You know where they are but they don't know where you are.

One little kid had gone around the end of his house, assuming that his Mom would follow him. His Mom went through the house and saw him from the window. He looked back over his shoulder and Mom wasn't there. For about three months after that he never let his Mom out of his sight.

This brings home to them in a very basic way, nonverbally, some of the basic existential elements of being a child.

"I really am dependent for my life on my mother and father. If I get too far away from them, I really am in danger of losing my life."

A child has to know this, just as they have to know that the parents are more powerful than they are. Otherwise they will engage in daredevil behavior.

It's an elemental fear. Parents know what that is. The child has to experience it under your tutelage in a titrated form so that it's manageable.

Become Unpredictable

Another way to Shake the Foundations is to become unpredictable. You forget things. They always think that parents are infallible. Mom could never forget lunch. Even if you just postpone it a half hour and then throw your hand on your face and say, "I forgot lunch!" they'll look at you real strangely, "How could you possibly—?" They'll start to think that maybe you're not all there.

You don't have to make any verbal connection; you don't have to say to the kid, "You made me so upset I forgot lunch." What you do is, you let their behavior go on at the time while you are forgetting to make lunch. That's all you have to do. They'll put two and two together. They can do the arithmetic. Body Logic!

"Motherrr, You Shouldn't Do That!"

Another Mom dealt with her four-year-old's tantrums in the supermarket in another way. The child was on the floor, screaming and kicking, and people were stopping to look. Mom heard them whispering, "Child abuse!"

"Shouldn't bring them shopping!"—you know the comments people make. Mom looked down at her child and said, "Gosh! That looks like so much fun, I think I'll do it myself!"

She was a good-sized lady, too, and she got down on the floor on her hands and knees and began tantruming, and her child got up in utter horror. She looked down at her mother and said in her most indignant tone, "Motherrr! You shouldn't *do* that!"

The kid kept a close eye on her Mom after that, looking out for any signs that Mother might be about to have a tantrum.

The Sound Of Splintering Wood

One of the Moms in our practice had a boy who was oversleeping and skipping school. One morning, while he was oversleeping upstairs, she went down in the basement and began kicking orange crates to bits, trampling on them. The sound of splintering wood went through the house, and the boy came downstairs, almost in tears, and he said, "Mom! Don't do that!! I'll go! I'll go!" It seemed to hit the sonic barrier for him. She had found something that was not child abuse but that the child could not tolerate, and that was the idea that his Mom might crack up, lose it, go out of control.

We recommend that you do it before you get desperate. You do it as a deliberate strategy. Once you've done something like that, then you can actually convey that kind of signal to a kid by just the arch of your eyebrow that indicates, "Gee, Mom is thinking about breaking up crates again!"

They will think very seriously about that, and there is nothing wrong with setting limits, because if you don't set them, the kid pushes further and further to find where the limits are. But just announcing limits verbally, that rarely cuts any ice.

You can learn some techniques that will suggest to the child the possibility that you might be getting close to the edge, that you might be getting ready to crack.

Mom and Dad can suddenly become angry at each other and have a fight with each other. If a child thinks that their behavior precipitated that fight between the parents, believe me, that's going to have consequences.

Use it sparingly. A little of this goes a long way.

One reason kids push so hard to find where the parents are going to finally take a stand, is that they have to know, "Am I the one who is really in charge around here? I don't even have impulse control!" They push and they push, "Where are they gonna stop? Where are they going to draw the line and make me straighten out?"

Drawing the Line

It's not a line in the sand. It's the line between what's real and not real. Reality is that parents could be driven too far. They could crack.

It's also the line of demarkation between parent and child, between the adult world and the world of the child. Parents have a life of their own. They come and go mysteriously, on missions of their own that have nothing to do with children. They have fun by themselves. They don't ask their children for permission. They don't explain. It wouldn't help anyway. The world of adults is not the world of childhood.

By having a life of their own and living it, grownups send really strong messages to their kids. The kids are set free from involvement in the life of their parents. They are freed from the false hope of controlling the grownups. The grownups are obviously taking care of themselves. The kids are free to be kids, to play, to grow up at their own pace.

13.

FUTURE PACING

What's Your Future?

Kids in middle school, even in high school, often have a lot of ambivalence about thinking about their future. Thinking ahead, planning for the future is not always to their taste. It's a big, confusing world out there. So I ask them, "Do you know what's going to happen after you've finished college and gotten your degree; and after you've finished Grad School and you've got your Ph.D, and after you've done a three-year Postdoctoral Fellowship and you're twenty-eight years old?"

They usually look at me in puzzlement and disbelief. And I say, "You're gonna start sending a check home every month for the rest of your life, to pay your poor old parents for supporting you all those years!"

And I wait a second or two and then I say, "That's what happens when you finish school. So don't ever quit school!"

They may have been planning to quit school early to play professional ball. It doesn't matter. They will hear your message and make the appropriate conclusions to fit their own life.

A Year Ahead

My older son started kindergarten a year early, so when he reached high school I told him, "You're a whole year ahead of yourself, so when you finish High School you're gonna have a whole year free to do whatever you want to do before you start in college."

He was absolutely delighted at getting this wonderful payoff for being a good student and finishing high school a year ahead of himself. And he chose to go to Europe with his high school band on a musical tour of Europe, giving concerts and traveling through the countries of Europe. But when they got to Yugoslavia, his passport was stolen and the Yugoslavian secret police picked him up and separated him from his fellow musicians. They took him alone on an airplane to Belgrade where they interrogated him; and when they finally released him and let him come home again he was a changed person. He was a mature young man. He was really ready to go to college, and he took it for granted that he was going to go to college, because we had taken it for granted.

We'll Wake You When It's Time

Parents of a child in my practice reported to me that after the first time their child came into their bedroom at night, they were planning to say, "OK, you can come in again. We'll wake you up when it's time."

If he wanted to be waked, they were going to wake him up out of a sound sleep and say, "It's time to come into our room now. We know you'd like to come in. It's time now."

He was happy with not being waked.

He slept through the whole night, till seven the next morning!

John Gall, MD, FAAP

Often It's Enough Just To Know That You've Got The Strategy

This is a point that is really significant. I don't know how to teach it. I really don't know how to get it across until you've actually had this experience, you won't believe me anyway. Often it's enough just to know that you've got the strategy, because kids have radar.

They will pick it up, they sense that something is different, and so they behave differently. You can talk in eight syllable words right over their head. You'd swear they can't understand a thing you're saying.

It Works Even If You Don't Buy It

It's like those electronic bedwetting alarms. I have recommended those on occasion and have had the kid sitting there with Dad or Mom listening as I explain to Dad how the thing works, and how the kid will not have to sleep in a wet bed, because the instant there's the slightest bit of moisture, the alarm will go off.

In one case, I didn't see the parents again for six months or so. I asked, "Oh, by the way, how did that alarm work?" They said, "We didn't buy it."

"Well, why not?" They said, "Well, it was nineteen dollars and we didn't want to buy it. We didn't want to pay for it. So we waited, and that night he didn't wet his bed. We waited another night, and he didn't wet his bed that night. We waited a week and he didn't wet his bed. A month later we decided we didn't need it."

It's amazing. This is a device that works even if you don't buy it.

That Magical First Hour of Life

When a young couple come to me for their first prenatal visit, I talk to them about that magical first hour after their baby is born. I explain how their baby sends out the first signals of readiness for human communication. I let them know how wonderful they are going to feel when their baby lets them know they are communicating well. Later, when they come in for their first postnatal visit, they tell me what a wonderful experience it was to communicate with a newborn baby, and how wonderful it was to know what they were doing.

It was their first experience, but through the magic of Future Pacing, they already knew how wonderful it would be.

14.

THE WAY THE WORLD IS

When a toddler starts to cruise around the house, the lowest three feet of the walls belong to him. I've recommended that architects design houses with three feet of washable crayon-board on every wall in every room.

It's different when teenagers decide to use public surfaces for their graffiti. Finally someone noticed that heavy stucco just doesn't appeal to graffiti artists. They go elsewhere.

Mall-rats, young people who hang around shopping malls all day, can't stand classical music. It drives them away more effectively than mosquito repellent or tear gas.

Both of these environmental strategies are in contrast with the "police control" approach that leaves the attractive nuisance in place and then punishes those who are attracted.

You can put an extra twist on an Environmental Strategy by forbidding whatever it is you want them to do. It adds spice to the achievement when they manage to frustrate you and do what you wanted them to do all along.

According to legend, the great musician Handel was forbidden by his parents to play the organ. To make sure he didn't, they put it in the attic. The little boy would wait until his parents were asleep and then sneak up to the attic and play on the organ for half the night.

Change the Environment If You Can

Why are electrical outlets placed so low on the baseboard that a baby can crawl over and get electrocuted? If all outlets were five feet up on the wall, we would not have this problem.

Electrical current of 110 volts at 60 cycles per second is just right for stopping the heart. Edison picked something that was convenient for him. He was not thinking about little kids when he designed it.

There's basically no attention paid to this kind of thing. The world is built for adults. The assumption is made that everybody knows self-protection in advance, and it's just not true. I think the best solution is to make it impossible for the child to get to those outlets.

This is Strategy Number One: If it's something in the environment that you can change, then change the environment.

Please Send Photo

Karen was afraid to be in her bed at night without Mom present. Mom put a large photo of herself in the bedroom where Karen could see it and Karen was quite satisfied.

Peeing in the Bathtub

Daniel, aged three and a half months, peed whenever he was put in the bath water; so, before giving him his bath, and while he still has his diaper on, Mom puts his feet in warm water. Daniel pees in his diaper, then Mom takes off his wet diaper and bathes him. He doesn't pee in the bath water because he has just peed and his bladder is empty.

A Paper to Pee On

Mary, three and a half years old, likes to pee on the floor. Dad started spreading newspapers around the house for her to pee on. Within twenty-four hours Mary stopped peeing on the floor. She commented, "I think I'll just use the potty."

June in December

Beth likes to wear her summer clothes to school even in the winter time. Beth puts on her summer outfit, and Mom puts her winter clothes on overtop of her summer clothes. Everybody's happy.

Juice Bar

Jon-Jon, sixteen months old, only wants to drink what he himself decides to drink. Mom keeps bottles of milk and juice in the refrigerator and lets him open the refrigerator door to look inside and choose for himself.

Impulse Control

There's a tradition in this country that everything is done by will power, that if you just put your mind to it, you can do it. But a child at the age of two does not have full impulse control. You may tell them that they will be severely punished if they do X but if they get the impulse to do X, it may just pop right out, even though they know they are going to be severely punished. So it obviously doesn't make sense to demand impulse control from a little person that doesn't have it.

Keep Your Body Between Them.

This is particularly important in regard to sibling rivalry, jealousy. A young couple told us that the first day they brought the new baby home, the older child toddled right up to the bassinet and in the flash of an eye he had two fingers out and aimed straight for the baby's eyes. And he had never even seen a baby before!! Something put that impulse there, and whammo! Out it came. They just barely pushed him out of the way in time.

Now, to scold a kid for that is utterly useless. He can't stop that impulse, or if he does it will be at the cost of a really traumatic prohibition, and still the impulse will come through, because at two years of age they don't have that control. So the way you handle that is with a modified form of Environmental Control. You keep your body between them at all times. If they are in the same room together, you are in that room and you are close enough that if the impulse pops out, you can just bump them, interrupt the movement so that they get pushed aside. You don't scold them, you don't punish them, you just bump 'em and they understand that one hundred percent. They know that you trust them completely, but you also know that they don't have impulse control and therefore they don't have to take upon themselves the impossible burden of trying to give you a behavioral sequence that they can't control.

Impulse Control is very unreliable. Some kids, after the first time they burn themselves, will have pretty good impulse control about fire, because they can see that it is hot. That's one of the first things. With a kid at age three, I wouldn't count on that very much. At age four, they may have control for a few simple things. What I'm suggesting is, you titrate it to the level of your own child's abilities, because if you ask them to perform at a level where they can't, it's just like that college course that was a little too tough for you. They're going to feel like a failure. So you stay at their level and take away from them that terrible burden of trying to perform above their ability.

The child gets a sense of security from knowing that the parents are in charge, and that a parent will physically restrain them from doing something that's bad. A lot of parents figure they'll traumatize their kid if they prevent them from doing something, but it's just the opposite. The child feels secure if they have the confidence that their parents will not let them do something out of bounds.

Providing a Secure Reality

When it becomes necessary to physically restrain a child, you just firmly and gently enfold them. You're not mad at them, you're not hurting them, but you are sending a very strong message to them that they do not have the power that belongs to adults, and that you can and will use your power to protect them from themselves.

If you take a toddler to Niagara Falls or to the Grand Canyon, you don't trust them to have impulse control. You have them in a little harness with a leather leash that clips on tight. If you are with them in a crowded international airport, you have them on a leash. You won't let them wander away and get kidnapped.

The Way The World Is

Environmental Control goes far beyond matters of safety and impulse control. You have the power to create a world of unquestioned assumptions for your child. If your house is full of books and they see you always reading, simple curiosity will drive them to look inside those books. They'll take it for granted that grownups read lots of books. They'll take it for granted that they are going to have a library in their own house when they grow up. That's just the way the world is.

15.

THE CHARLEY BROWN APPROACH

Just Wait For The Next Level Of Development

With kids, if you wait long enough, they move to the next higher level of development, so that the old stuff is no longer an issue, because they've just left it behind.

So you can just wait. Waiting is a very powerful strategy. If you have a problem that you just can't solve, don't give up. Just wait, and after a certain number of months or years, that problem may be gone—and you will have another one!

If you decide to just wait, you have to make sure you really let it go. No nagging!

If it still doesn't go away, you may need to ask yourself if it's really a problem. Maybe it's really your own problem. Or if it's a big problem, you may need to ask an expert for some help. Waiting is just one strategy. It's not suitable for everything.

Ride the Sine Curve

No matter how problematic, even abnormal their behavior seems, remember, almost every human behavior tends to wax and wane over time, and if you have the courage, you can ride that curve until it hits the peak and starts to come down again. You don't have to confront them. You can just let them ride. Then they will know that you actually have faith in them, that you really do trust that their self-regulatory mechanisms work.

It's a good attitude for your own survival, too, as a parent. Not everything needs fixing.

16.

FOR EXPERTS ONLY (THE BIG NO-NO's)

Things not to do unless you really know how to use them constructively:

1. Nagging (the repetition of unsuccessful requests).

Nag them to do what you want them to *stop* doing!

2. Bribery

The price keeps going up, and anyway, it's an attempt to reward behavior that hasn't happened yet. But an unexpected reward is *not* a bribe. Bring them a dish of ice cream while they are hard at work studying their homework. Don't announce it in advance—just show up with the ice cream.

3. Accusations.

Don't do this to a child—it's dirty fighting. The more they deny your accusations, the less convincing they are to themselves. The child will end up believing there must be a grain of truth in the accusations and he just can't see it—thereby destroying his trust in his own perceptions.

Constructive use of Accusation usually involves the element of humor or irony.

"Sneaking off to do your homework again, eh? How many times have I told you to go outside and play and leave your homework to the last minute like any normal kid?"

4. Attributions (*You're* the one who...)

These are accusations at an even higher level of sneakiness—taken for granted as just a fact of life. Who can defend themselves against *that*? But that doesn't mean the victim can't respond. A child can become hopeless about the possibility of change, can accept himself as a flawed inferior being, or even embrace with exasperated enthusiasm a negative career based on the attributions leveled against them.

It's possible to use Attribution in a constructive way: "You always have such good ideas."

"I knew I could count on you."

But you need to be especially careful to avoid labeling and role-casting, such as: "You are the smart one in the family." That sounds positive but has hidden implications that can make trouble later.

"I Used To Think She Was Stubborn But Now I Know She's Just Lazy"

We had a mom who brought her child in at 6 weeks and said, "I used to think that she was stubborn, but now I know she's just lazy." Six weeks old and already labelled!

This was a breast feeding baby, and that was the mother's assessment of this child's breastfeeding behavior.

"Stubborn" meant that the mother couldn't get the responses that she wanted. Then she was able to change that to the concept "lazy," which meant the child wasn't deliberately frustrating her, it was just a slow responder and was lazy. She probably had one other term in her verbal model and that would have been "a good baby"—which is one that would spontaneously do what she wanted. That is a verbal model that's too simple, it's got too few distinctions in it.

If you see "stubborness" then you're naturally going to expect certain things. You're going to act in certain ways, you're going to get an interaction started that assumes this. And within two or three years the child will know in their heart that they are "stubborn" or "stupid" or whatever, and so will you. Don't do this!

He's Already Been Good To Me

One teenage unwed mother in the hospital announced to me when I came in, the morning after the baby was born, "He's already been good to me!"

"He's already been good to me". At that tender age she was interpreting his behavior in terms of altruism and selfishness—very adult ideas, I guess you would say, or at least ideas that would be more appropriate for a 3 year old or 4 year old.

The Language Problem

That opens a whole Pandora's box. It's hard to believe, but every language that the human race has ever used suffers from a serious flaw. The structure of all languages almost without exception is such that you can make an attribution about the other person. "He is just lazy."

But what does it mean when you say a person is "just lazy?" or "just stubborn?" It really means that you have tried out some of your repertoire of behavioral interventions in order to elicit a desired piece of behavior from the other person and you have failed, because your repertoire was too limited.

91

What you ought to say under those circumstances is, "I lack sufficient repertoire to elicit this desired behavior X from person Y." Instead of that you say, "He's just stubborn." We put the blame on the other person, rather than recognizing what we should, that it's our lack of repertoire, not the other person's character defect, that's involved.

Every language in the world enables you to do this little maneuver that puts the blame on somebody else. If we think a child is doing something called "misbehaving," it's worth remembering that the behavior that a person exhibits is elicited in part by the surroundings, and therefore in theory it should be modifiable by changes in his surroundings. Since we're the most important element in the surroundings for a child, it really means, "Here's a challenge. Our repertoire up till now has not succeeded. Would there be some other items of repertoire that might succeed?"

The common consensus has it, that there is only one way to deal with a child and that is to be firm, consistent, nurturing, to be fair and to be clear, to explain everything, and then if they still don't do it, send them to the reformatory or the insane asylum, or whatever! Because now *they* are the ones that are to blame; the fault is in *them*. But if you have more than one strategy in your repertoire, if you can switch from one strategy to another over a sufficiently wide range, then you'll discover that you can in fact produce amazing changes, that you would never have thought possible.

5. Explanations.

Any explanation more than five words long is too long. Children don't have that much Verbal Model to work with.

"Moms don't do homework when you're twelve."

However, a long-winded explanation can sometimes be used to achieve a constructive goal. (Use with caution)

6. Ex Cathedra demands.

"Do it because I said so."
Want your child to give up thinking? This will do it.
"Give up your will. Submit to mine—because I'm bigger."

Again, constructive use of this strategy is possible: "Open your mouth and close your eyes and I'll give you a nice surprise." (Be sure it really is a nice surprise.)

7. "Not-Doing" Something.

In general, this is impossible. Provide an acceptable alternate pathway. If you are tempted to say, "Don't sit there dawdling over your homework all night," you can say instead, "You don't need to bother doing your homework tonight. You can do it in the morning while waiting for the bus."

8. Indirect Verbal Attacks

Certain specific phrases should immediately raise a red flag of warning in your mind. Examples:

1. "If you really…";
2. "Even *you* should…"
3. "We all understand why you…"
4. "A person who…"
5. "Why don't you ever…"
6. "Some people would…"
7. "Don't you even care…"

It's probably wise never to use such language with your child. For the complete list, including effective counters, see:

John Gall, MD, FAAP

Elgin, Suzette Haden (1980). The Gentle Art of Verbal Self-Defense. New York. Prentice-Hall.

17.

IS THAT ALL?

Are there really only fifteen different types of strategies available for human interaction? I doubt it. True, most of the strategies I have learned to recognize fall into one or more of the categories presented here, but some don't.

The harder you think about these strategies, the more they tend to merge. Maybe they are all examples of one great strategy with (as yet) no name. Call it the Dance of Human Interaction.

What is important is not the name but the patient accumulation of specific strategies until you have a constructive response for almost any situation. You rarely have to fall back into Default Mode. Then you can feel that you have mastered the Performing Art of Parenting.

The Use and Misuse of Humor

Underlying all of the strategies is an element of playfulness, of good humor, a tacit implication that human interaction is a game, a dance, a playful thing that is deeply satisfying in itself and rarely if ever needs to descend down to the level of confrontation and grim alternatives. That basic attitude is revealed in the tone of humor that pervades the strategies.Humor itself, the use of a funny twist on the situation, is thus a kind of higher-level strategy, one that adds potency to the strategies where it is a component.

Obviously, humor doesn't mean discounting real issues or making fun of your child. You are showing him that you, too, know how to dance the dance of human interaction; that you, too, are a child at heart.

18.

GUIDING PRINCIPLES

1. Learn To Pay Attention To Feedback.

Without feedback you don't know what effect you are having.

2. Learn Problem Location.

It's not cricket to ask the child to change if the problem is basically your own.

3. Switch Strategies Freely.

If at first you don't succeed, give up. Do something else. Switch to a different strategy. Don't waste energy pushing interventions that aren't working.

4. Nonverbal Modelling Is Usually Better Than Verbal.

Never do explicitly what you can do implicitly. The child's verbal model of the universe is extremely crude. (So is ours—just a little less so!) Use behavior—or as Beth Gall says, "Behavior Behavior".

5. Don't Explain Everything.

It's easy to give away your power by talking. There are times when it's better not to explain. Your interventions are much more powerful if they don't know what's going to happen. Build anticipation. That way, you will have their full attention.

6. Learn To Be Actors And Actresses.

After you have learned your lines and used them successfully three times, you won't be "acting" any more.

7. Learn More Lines! (Requisite Variety)

Increase Your Repertoire. The more strategies you have at your fingertips the better equipped you will be to meet any situation. The Principle Of Requisite Variety states that in any System, control is exercised by the element with the greatest variety of behavioral responses.

8. Learn Verbal Pacing.

"You *don't* want to clean up your room. You *want* to go out and play." Validate their position. That way, they will know that you really understand the situation.

9. If You Don't Want It To Be In Their Repertoire, Don't Talk About It.

Why give them an explicit verbal model of things you don't want them to do? You just give them practice in doing in fantasy what you don't want them to do. Don't talk about "avoiding juvenile delinquency," "staying out of trouble", etc. They know how you feel about such things.

10. Minimize Constraints.

Take a good look at what you're asking, and why. The child may be merely trying to stay out of your overly rigid system. Be selective. Ignore unimportant stuff.

In raising a child, an ounce of spontaneity is worth a pound of obedience.

11. Don't Get Polarized. Stay Flexible.

Trench warfare is self-defeating. Everybody loses.

12. Stay Out Of The Fairness Trap.

As a parent, you are obligated to provide to each child what that child needs. A new baby needs more attention than an older sibling. As a parent, you decide who needs what and how much, and you cannot be blackmailed by complaints of unfairness. It's unequal but it's not unfair!

13. Parents Should Take Care Of Their Own "Child" Needs First.

Parents have needs for security, comfort, validation, rest, recreation, etc. Don't try to get these from the child. That turns the world upside down and stands things on their head.

14. Learn To Get In Touch With The Kid Part Of Yourself And Use That Part In Communicating With Your Children.

Learn to play. Learn to dance.

15. Use Natural Consequences, Not Punishment.

Don't be a victim. Let the child's failure to learn the desired responses get in his way, not yours. Punishing a child teaches him to punish others.

16. Praise The Achievement, Don't Criticize The Shortcoming.

Children always do poorly at first what they later will do well. If you criticize the shortcoming you merely discourage them and fixate their behavior at the level of poor performance.

17. Let The Child Have As Much Control As She Or He Can Handle Without Feeling Overwhelmed.

Remember, the reason you are doing all these things is so *you* can have a feeling of being in control. Why not let him enjoy that, too, in his way and at his level?

18. Don't Ask For Performances.

Some kids are little hams and will repeat their latest achievements on request. Most kids don't like this and won't do it. You'll save yourself a lot of grief if you just don't ask them to perform.

19. Utilize The Spontaneous Offerings Of The Child.

That's the behavior they already know how to do, the behavior they are already exhibiting. Find a way to put it to good use.

20. If Your Child's Behavior Seems Malicious Or Crazy, Remember That This Means A Basic Miscommunication Has Occurred Somewhere.

Or else there is actually craziness somewhere, either in the family or the school, or *somewhere*. Make it your assignment to find out where the problem is. Don't ask, find out for yourself.

21. Respect Inborn Temperament.

Let them be how they grow, even if it's a little strange.

22. Respect Infant Preferences.

Preferences start at birth. Pay attention to their preferences. They'll love you for it.

23. Respect The Developmental Level Of The Child.

a. "Lying" versus reality testing. If there's a bear in the bathroom, deal with the bear, don't give a sermon on lying.
b. Impulse control. When it's developmentally not there, don't try to elicit it. Keep sibs physically apart.
c. Autonomic control (sphincters, etc.) Same idea. When it's developmentally not there, don't try to elicit it.
d. Sharing. First comes possession, then comes sharing! Give them time—lots of time! Like eight or ten years! Would you be willing to share your new sports car?

101

24. Anticipate And Encourage A Relapse.

Understand that a relapse may be a signal that you have made a successful intervention. They are escalating their old responses to find out what went wrong, why the old methods aren't working… Then they can frustrate you by not having a relapse.

25. Understand That Learning Proceeds By Fits And Starts.

Sudden advances are followed by long periods of little change. And often the first indication that a major advance is about to take place is the occurrence of restless, irritable behavior—the Learning Tantrum.

26. You Are Always Fundamentally On Their Side.

If you are not for them, then who is for them? And if not now, when?

27. Help Them To Move To The Next Higher Level of Development.

Your task as a parent is to help them get past the sticky points, to facilitate their own mastery of their current developmental tasks and so to move on to the next developmental level.

28. Set Them Up To Succeed Whenever Possible.

That sweet feeling of success, of competency: we all need it. They do, too. The more they get it, the more competent and successful they feel. The more they feel it, the more competent and successful they become. It snowballs.

29. Don't Give Away Your Power Unless That's Part Of Your Strategy.

Don't negotiate with a child who is too young to negotiate. A two-year old has a very rudimentary idea of the meaning of compromise, much less of promise, contract, obligation. Forget it! On the other hand, they often do understand barter (exchange).

30. Learn To Deliberately Use Your Own Failure And Powerlessness.

Allow children to succeed in getting the better of you by doing what you really wanted them to do all along.

31. Learn to Make A *Little* Change.

It will snowball.

32. Learn Timing.

Learn *when* to make your move to have the best effect.

John Gall, MD, FAAP

REFERENCES

(1) Erickson, Milton H.(1958). "Pediatric hypnotherapy." *The American Journal of Clinical Hypnosis* 1, 25-29.
(2) Campbell, Joseph (1988). The Power of Myth. New York. Doubleday. p.118.
(3) Elgin, Suzette Haden (1980). The Gentle Art of Verbal Self-Defense. New York. Prentice-Hall.

John Gall, MD, FAAP

INDEX

N

O

P

R

S

T

ABOUT THE AUTHOR

John Gall, M.D., was educated at St. John's College in Annapolis, Maryland, George Washington University in Washington, D.C., and at Yale College. After receiving his medical training at George Washington University School of Medicine, he trained in Pediatrics at the Mayo Clinic. He has been a Fellow of the American Academy of Pediatrics since 1958. He retired from private practice in 2001 after more than forty years of experience in behavioral and developmental problems of children.

Printed in the United States
29624LVS00001B/80

9 781410 723178